The Meditation and Mindfulness Edge

Teachers juggle a lot, so the ability to stay focused, calm, and mentally sharp is critical. This generous and heartfelt book shows you how meditation and mindfulness practices can enable you to not only survive but flourish in the classroom. Dr. Lisa Klein presents powerful findings on the effects of meditation on teachers. She reveals the positive effects that meditation had on her and her own career in education. She also shares personal stories that demonstrate how meditation may offer a balm to help teachers stay healthy mentally and physically while tapping into higher levels of awareness, including experiences of self-actualization and synchronicity. In addition, she offers practical, simple strategies for both developing teacher presence and shifting to a more positive classroom energy. This powerful book moves beyond basic self-care tools to help you develop a new, lifelong practice. Anyone involved in education can benefit from this book, as can anyone interested in learning more about how meditation can help with health and well-being in general.

Lisa M. Klein, Ed.D., is a certified meditation teacher and has been teaching meditation privately and conducting workshops since 2003—introducing people of all ages to the power of meditation. In addition to teaching both Vedic and mindfulness meditation, Lisa taught high school English for over 20 years. Visit her website at www.lisakleinmindfulness.com.

Also Available by Routledge Eye On Education
(www.routledge.com/k-12)

Embracing Adult SEL: An Educator's Guide to Personal Social Emotional Learning Success
Wendy Turner

Everyday Self-Care for Educators: Tools and Strategies for Well-Being
Carla Tantillo Philibert, Christopher Soto, Lara Veon

Teach from Your Best Self: A Teacher's Guide to Thriving in the Classroom
Jay Schroder

Dear Teacher: 100 Days of Inspirational Quotes and Anecdotes
Brad Johnson and Hal Bowman

365 Quotes for Teachers: Inspiration and Motivation for Every Day of the Year
Danny Steele

First Aid for Teacher Burnout, Second Edition: How You Can Find Peace and Success
Jenny Rankin

The Meditation and Mindfulness Edge
Becoming a Sharper, Healthier, and Happier Teacher

Lisa M. Klein

Routledge
Taylor & Francis Group
NEW YORK AND LONDON

Designed cover image: © Sandra Clegg / Getty Images

First published 2024
by Routledge
605 Third Avenue, New York, NY 10158

and by Routledge
4 Park Square, Milton Park, Abingdon, Oxon, OX14 4RN

Routledge is an imprint of the Taylor & Francis Group, an informa business

© 2024 Lisa M. Klein

The right of Lisa M. Klein to be identified as author of this work has been asserted in accordance with sections 77 and 78 of the Copyright, Designs and Patents Act 1988.

All rights reserved. No part of this book may be reprinted or reproduced or utilised in any form or by any electronic, mechanical, or other means, now known or hereafter invented, including photocopying and recording, or in any information storage or retrieval system, without permission in writing from the publishers.

Trademark notice: Product or corporate names may be trademarks or registered trademarks, and are used only for identification and explanation without intent to infringe.

ISBN: 978-1-032-50267-0 (hbk)
ISBN: 978-1-032-49817-1 (pbk)
ISBN: 978-1-003-39766-3 (ebk)

DOI: 10.4324/9781003397663

Typeset in Palatino
by SPi Technologies India Pvt Ltd (Straive)

For my family

Contents

List of Figures ix
Meet the Author x
Acknowledgements xi

Introduction 1

Part I
UNDERSTANDING MEDITATION AND ITS BENEFITS 7

1 What Is Meditation and Mindfulness? 9

2 Why Should We Care about the Well-Being of
  Teachers? 18

3 Effects of Meditation on the Body and Mind 30

4 The Effects of Meditation on Teachers 48

5 Critiques and Caveats about Meditation and
  Mindfulness 60

Part II
**STORIES FROM MY CAREER AND HOW MEDITATION
PLAYED A VITAL ROLE** 69

6 The Transformation of an Introvert: How Meditation
  Calmed My Anxiety and Helped Me to Blossom 71

7 The Early Years of Teaching 79

8 From Fear to Love: More Stories from the Early
   Years. 87

9 Surviving a Toxic Workplace: How Meditation
   Shielded Me from the Negative Effects of
   Co-Worker Tensions. 97

10 Synchronicity. 104

11 Training for the Worst 110

12 Dr. Mom, the Vampire 117

13 A Call to Action that Was Guided by Synchronicity. . . . 124

14 Reflections on My Career and Meditation. 130

Part III
**SHIFTING YOUR ENERGY: SIMPLE STRATEGIES TO
INTRODUCE MINDFULNESS INTO YOUR LIFE NOW 135**

15 Shifting Your Energy and the Energy of Your
   Classroom. 137

16 Suggestions for Learning to Meditate and
   Incorporating a Mindfulness Program into
   a School or Workplace 148

Figures

12.1 Yearbook photo of author taken in 1997, during her first year of teaching. 119

12.2 Photo of author taken in 2021. Photograph by Becky Thurner Braddock 119

Meet the Author

Lisa M. Klein (MS.Ed., MSc, Ed.D.) has dedicated her life to teaching and meditating. She began her training in meditation at the age of 19 and has been meditating ever since. For over 20 years, she taught high school English while teaching meditation privately and conducting workshops on mindfulness and meditation. In 2008, she completed her doctorate at Duquesne University, focusing her research on the effects of meditation on teachers. As a high school English teacher, department chair, and university instructor, Dr. Klein witnessed the high levels of stress and teacher burnout of her colleagues as well as the growing number of students who suffer from stress and anxiety. This realization led her out of the classroom to completing a Master of Science in Mindfulness Studies at the University of Aberdeen in Scotland. She now dedicates her life to teaching meditation full-time. In addition to being a teacher of Vedic meditation, she is certified to teach mindfulness meditation through the Mindfulness Association of the UK.

Outside of teaching, she loves spending time with her family and being in nature. Her philosophy of the earth and all of its inhabitants being interconnected has been shaped by both her meditation practice and her time spent studying abroad.

Visit her website at www.lisakleinmindfulness.com.

Acknowledgements

I must start at the beginning of this lifetime and give my heartfelt gratitude to my family for their infinite support, love, and encouragement. To my great-grandparents, grandparents, parents, and my brother for being my first and forever cheerleaders.

I am beyond grateful for my husband, Jason, and his infinite support of all my adventures. He is a man who makes everything possible and, in a truly selfless way, has enabled me to flourish on my own path. He embodies a self-actualized mindset as he lives life unencumbered by his ego. His critical eye and countless revisions of this book have encouraged my voice to take shape and to fly courageously. Jason is my sounding board, my editor, my meditation and life partner, and my rock. How can I keep from singing?

To my children, Liam and Karina, who have supported me with great patience, encouragement, and love as I've completed this book. May you both continue to bring music and light into this world.

I send infinite gratitude to my meditation group and my meditation teacher, who have been with me and supported me in body, mind, and spirit for 30 years.

Being a firm believer in the power of "being in the flow" of life, I am grateful that the universe led me to the MSc in Studies of Mindfulness at the University of Aberdeen, where I was able to meet and work with many remarkable people, including Colette Savage and Dr. Graeme Nixon.

I would also like to thank the Mindfulness Association, which has provided me with practical, approachable ways to bring mindfulness instruction to a broader audience.

I must likewise acknowledge and give thanks to all my students, who have been some of my greatest teachers.

Thank you to Lauren Davis and Routledge, Taylor & Francis Group publishing, who have provided me with this wonderful opportunity to share my stories and my passion for teaching and for meditation.

To all of the people who have magically joined me on my journey at the precise time I needed them throughout my life—some for just a moment, some for a short time, and some for eternity—thank you for your guidance and help in getting me to this moment.

Introduction

You meditate? You teach mindfulness? What's that, some kind of woke BS?

Uh. No. Not quite. It's 5,000 years old. So. You know. Not exactly *woke*.

Yeah, well, it sounds like wokeness BS to me.

I've had all sorts of responses from people over the years regarding meditation. This response was one of my favorites. A couple of years ago, I was getting my hair done, and the guy who does my hair had another client there hanging out. I broke my old rule. When she asked me what I do for a living, I decided to tell her. A perfect stranger, and that was her response. There was no shifting her focus off the mindset that it must be a woke thing. Years ago, I just never talked about meditation to anybody. Then I started to open up more and more about it with co-workers and family and friends. But, honestly, sometimes it still feels exhausting trying to explain it and trying to justify why I practice and teach it.

Allow Me to Dispel Five Misconceptions about Meditation

Misconception #1: I don't have a personality that would fit in with being a meditator.

I speak my mind, and I'm not good at just accepting problems. If I don't like something, I'm going to tell you about it. I'm not a calm, chill kind of person. Meditating will make me too "soft," "too spacey." I need to be tough for my job. I need to be sharp and straightforward because I deal with a lot of crap. If my head is too much in the clouds and I become wishy-washy, then I'm going to look weak and people will take advantage of me. I'm not going to be as successful at my job, because I won't have that competitive edge.

Reality: Yes, meditation can make you very relaxed, and you may even experience times when you will feel blissful, especially after long-term meditation practice. Paradoxically, however, meditation will make you sharper, more intuitive, and more insightful and give you greater clarity and awareness. Meditation practice will increase your ability to detect dishonesty and enable you to read a room better. By meditating, your problem-solving and creative abilities will grow, so that instead of having to react to problems, you will be able to respond to them with greater precision. Your responses to situations will also become more objective, accurate, and beneficial. You may even be able to head off the problem before it even surfaces. So, no, meditation won't take away your competitive edge. It will sharpen your edge considerably.

Misconception #2: I don't have time to meditate.

Reality: You don't have time NOT to meditate.

Meditating for 20 minutes is like taking a two-hour nap. That's a good return on your investment. More importantly, when you come out of meditating, you feel an alert restfulness unlike the feeling of grogginess that is usually experienced after taking a nap. In fact, you might even require less sleep when you meditate every day. You'll spend less time rehashing past events and less time frozen in fear about the future. Meditating makes you more efficient. There are a fixed number of hours in a day. Meditating will help you use them to your best advantage.

Misconception #3: I can't meditate, because I can't shut off my mind. My head won't shut up!

Reality: Nobody has an "off" switch in the back of their head that can just be clicked off. *Weird.* And, actually, thank goodness because that would be yet another thing we would all walk around worrying about! "OMG! I hope nobody comes up to me and switches off my brain!"

Meditation doesn't click off your brain so that thoughts stop. If you have ever tried meditating and gave up because you still had thoughts going on in your mind, you need to try meditation again. And make sure you have a certified teacher who can provide you with one-on-one, personalized assistance. A good meditation teacher will guide you through the process of training your mind to allow the thoughts *to be* without becoming inundated by them. You will begin to develop the skill of being able to reduce the incessant chatter in your mind. Your habituated tendency to become distracted by your thoughts will begin to lessen.

Misconception #4: I'm a caregiver. I can't be so self-indulgent to make time for myself every day to meditate. I have to take care of my kids. I have to take care of my elderly parents. I can't take time away from them and focus on myself.

Reality: By helping yourself, you're helping others. When you meditate, you not only affect yourself, you also affect your environment and the people around you. You can actually shift the energy of your house, and over time, your family will begin to notice the subtle changes not only in your demeanor but in the atmosphere of your home. Meditating helps to foster more present-moment awareness and leads to greater patience, compassion, and kindness. These qualities are essential for any caregiver. By taking care of yourself, you will be able to take better care of others.

Misconception #5: I'm religious, and I don't want meditation to interfere with my religious beliefs. *Or*: I'm not religious, and I don't want to do anything related to religion.

Reality: While many religions, including Christianity, Judaism, Buddhism, and Islam, have their own forms of meditative practice, the type of meditation and mindfulness that this book is discussing is a secularized form of meditation. We must acknowledge that mindfulness has its origins in a Zen Buddhist tradition, for instance, but we don't need to practice or adhere to the dogma of Buddhism in order to practice mindfulness. With a secular focus on meditation, we are looking at the scientific evidence that shows the many physical and mental health benefits of meditation and how meditation can have positive effects within our personal and professional lives.

Whom Is This Book For?

Anybody who is interested in improving their life, being healthier, happier, more creative, and tapping into their full potential will gain something from this book. Specifically, this book looks through the lens of being a teacher and how meditation can affect teachers; however, these insights can be applied to other career fields as well.

What Kind of Book Is This?

It's part research, part storytelling, and part tips and suggestions. It's about personal growth and maximizing your potential through the practice of meditation.

What Kind of Book Is This Not?

It's not a "how to meditate" instructional guide. You need a real person who is a certified, highly trained, and well-practiced teacher to properly learn how to meditate. Just like you can read about learning how to drive a car in a book, you can read about learning how to meditate from a book. But, after reading the driving manual, you need to get your butt in a car with an actual driving instructor. Same with meditating. I'm showing you what meditation can do for you in this book, which will hopefully entice you to get out and find a qualified meditation teacher.

How This Book is Arranged

There are three parts to this book. The first part is informational and research-based. It gives an overview of the definitions of meditation and mindfulness and then a provides a rationale and introduction to why meditation can be helpful to teachers. It also presents some of the research and findings of meditation in relation to mental and physical health along with findings on the effects of meditation on classroom teachers. Notably, there is also a chapter within this part of the book that discusses the caveats of meditation and mindfulness and presents some of the ethical considerations that are frequently overlooked by schools and advocates of mindfulness programs.

The second part of this book takes an autoethnographic perspective and analyzes my 23-year journey as a teacher who practiced meditation. This section of the book is divided into vignettes from the beginning, middle, and end of my career as a high school English teacher at a large, diverse school. The narratives are raw and honest in their accounts of my teaching experiences. A mixture of laughter, fear, love, sadness, and hope, these narratives demonstrate the poignant reality of being a teacher in America today and how meditation may offer a balm to help teachers stay healthy mentally and physically while tapping into higher levels of awareness, including experiences of self-actualization and synchronicity.

The third part of this book provides simple strategies for both developing presence and shifting to a more positive energy in either your classroom or place of work. Suggestions for finding an appropriate and qualified meditation teacher/mindfulness program are discussed for those who are interested in learning to meditate. Ethical considerations and trauma-informed mindfulness will be revisited here for those who are interested in incorporating mindfulness in their classrooms, schools, or other work settings.

May this book leave the reader with a sense of how meditation can benefit teachers and people of all walks of life by attributing to

- ♦ Improved mental and physical health and well-being
- ♦ Creativity and problem-solving skills
- ♦ Compassion
- ♦ Higher levels of awareness

This book is my offering not only to teachers but to people in any field who have experienced stress, feelings of being overwhelmed, or feelings of anxiety and worry or to anyone who just wants to find ways to be healthier and happier.

Part I
Understanding Meditation and Its Benefits

1

What Is Meditation and Mindfulness?

What's the Difference Between Meditation and Mindfulness?

For about 30 years, I've been meditating, and I am part of a wonderful meditation group. This group of lifelong meditators has dedicated their life to practicing and teaching meditation. We practice a form of Vedic meditation. My fellow meditators are highly disciplined people from all walks of life who meditate twice a day and walk the walk of a meditator through their words and actions. They have dedicated their lives to bringing the fruits of meditation into their daily existence and various careers, including working as engineers, nurses, computer software techies, steel mill workers, business owners, teachers, real estate agents, musicians, financial analysts, designers, therapists, and sales and marketing professionals. They are real-life examples of harnessing the power of meditation to achieve personal and professional success, harmony, and happiness.

When the buzzword of mindfulness started to become more and more prolific, many of my fellow meditators—and, yes, this includes myself—were skeptical. From what we could tell, it seemed like a watered-down, fast-food type of approach to what meditation is. Why would somebody want to waste their time learning and practicing mindfulness when they could just learn how to meditate? Meditation brought deep, long-lasting results. Mindfulness seemed too trendy, informal, trite, and gimmicky. Then I began to contemplate that although there may be the Dollar Store variety of mindfulness that seemed to be infiltrating the collective consciousness of society in the same way that the "Keep Calm and Carry On" British World War II slogan had become morphed into anything from "Keep Calm and Eat Cupcakes" to "Keep Calm and Go Shopping," there must also be more authentic, beneficial forms of mindfulness.

In teaching mainstream audiences how to meditate, I realized that I needed to further explore exactly what this mindfulness trend was. I wanted to be prepared to answer questions pertaining to the difference between meditation and mindfulness. Because I taught high school at the time, I also wanted to learn practices that I could share with my students. (The Vedic form of meditation that I teach requires the student to be at least 18 years old.) Therefore, I was determined to dive into the belly of the beast and not only study mindfulness but really research it on deeper level. I didn't just want to get a certification in mindfulness. I wanted to know it more intimately and in a way that would legitimize my path into mindfulness. I decided to study and research mindfulness at the graduate level.

I had been practicing meditation for 26 years and had been teaching meditation for 16 years when I decided to become a student again and get a Master of Science degree in Mindfulness Studies. The first classes were held at the Kagyu Samye Ling Tibetan Buddhist Monastery in Eskdalemuir, Scotland. After a long journey, I arrived in the beautiful countryside of Scotland eager to embrace the "beginner's mind" and learn about different forms of meditation and mindfulness techniques. Learning, however, is not always neat and tidy, beautifully packaged with clear answers. As students from all over the U.K. and Europe (I was one of two students from the United States) sat in the lecture hall and listened to the Tibetan Buddhist monk who was introducing us to mindfulness, I had an urge to ask, "What is the difference between meditation and mindfulness?" I had even written the question down in my notebook, so I wouldn't forget to ask it later. I wanted to ask it right away, to blurt it out, but was hesitant to break the tone of acquiescence and quiet acceptance that was in the room.

Just then a more brazen student asked the monk, "Can you please explain to us the difference between meditation and mindfulness?" Nervous laughter filled the room. Aha! I was not the only one pondering this. Apparently, many students (including those who had practiced meditation previously) also wanted clarification. Collectively, we leaned in to hear the response. The Tibetan Buddhist monk also laughed a bit as he struggled to have an exact answer for us. Then another instructor jumped in, saying that mindfulness creates the condition for meditation to occur. This led to more questions. A few students offered their thoughts. No concrete answer was arrived at in this session, and ultimately, we left with the task of allowing the answer to emerge in due time.

As you can see, even experienced meditators struggle to answer the question of *What is the difference between mindfulness and meditation?* The two terms "meditation" and "mindfulness" are often used interchangeably, but should they be? The Mindfulness Association of the U.K. provides a possible clarification: "We can be mindful at any time throughout our day, however, meditation is the deliberate act of intending to be mindful. Mindfulness meditation might involve sitting quietly on a chair or cushion."[1] John P. Miller, author, professor, and advocate of meditation in education, explains that "[m]indfulness can be seen as meditation in action."[2] Rob Nairn, who examines the psychology of meditation, believes that "[t]he continual practice of meditation causes mindfulness to grow—just as training with weights causes muscles to grow."[3] These explanations resonate with me because the more I meditate, the more I feel grounded in the present moment, the more aware and mindful I feel about my surroundings and what I'm experiencing in the moment throughout my day.

The Informal and Formal Sides of Mindfulness

There exist many different types of mindfulness and meditation techniques. When comparing different methods of mindfulness and meditation, you might find it helpful to first acknowledge that there are both informal and formal techniques of mindfulness. Typically, informal mindfulness techniques are shorter (maybe only a few minutes), can be done anywhere, require less training, and help us to bring our attention into our daily activities in a real-time type of way, even helping us during a moment of crisis. Formal mindfulness techniques tend to be longer in duration (20–30 minutes usually), require more training/guidance, and aid us in our long-term development of mindfulness (Table 1.1).

Jon Kabat-Zinn, who is credited with bringing secular mindfulness to the West and who created the MBSR (Mindfulness-Based Stress Reduction) program, explains that mindfulness is "paying attention in a particular way: on purpose, in the present moment, and nonjudgmentally."[5] Succinctly put, "Mindfulness is the opposite of distraction."[6] Additionally, mindfulness enables us to become more aware, less reactive, more accepting, and more focused on the present moment.[7] Table 1.2 delineates a few of the many definitions of mindfulness, which have certain shared viewpoints.

In reviewing Table 1.2, you may notice several commonalities in the different definitions of mindfulness. Concepts such as present moment awareness and acceptance/not judging what is happening in the moment are found through each of the definitions.

TABLE 1.1 A few examples of informal and formal mindfulness practices

Examples of Informal Mindfulness Practices	Examples of Formal Mindfulness Practices
♦ Mindful eating ♦ Short breathing exercises ♦ Self-Compassion Break (developed by Kristen Neff)[4] ♦ Bringing your full attention into your daily activities	♦ Sitting mindfulness meditation ♦ Body Scan ♦ Mindful movement, such as yoga-based mindful movement, Qigong, or mindful walking

TABLE 1.2 A few definitions of mindfulness

Author/Speaker	Mindfulness Definition
Jon Kabat-Zinn (1994)	"paying attention in a particular way: on purpose, in the present moment, and nonjudgmentally"[8]
Rick Hanson and Richard Mendius (2009)	"Mindfulness just means being fully aware of something, in the moment with it, and not judging or resisting it."[9]
Rob Nairn (2001)	"Knowing what is happening, while it is happening, no matter what it is"[10]
Choden (2019)	Mindfulness is about remembering: "In Buddhism, it's about remembering the teachings of the Buddha and remembering to apply it.... In a secular context, it's more about remembering to fully inhabit the present moment and all that entails."[11]
Christopher K. Germer (2009)	"Mindfulness has a quality of *being in the now*, a sense of freedom, of perspective, of being connected, not judging, of flowing through the day. When we're mindful, we're less likely to want life to be other than it is, at least for the moment."[12]
Yongey Mingyur Rinpoche (2007)	"learning to simply rest in a bare awareness of thoughts, feelings, and perceptions as they occur"[13]

A Closer Look at Meditation

Now let's take a look at some explanations of meditation. The Dalai Lama clarifies,

> Meditation is the process whereby we gain control over the mind and guide it in a more virtuous direction. Meditation may be thought of as a technique by which we diminish the force of old thought habits and develop new ones.[14]

According to Daniel Goleman, an expert in the field of meditation in relation to psychology and behavioral sciences,

> Meditation trains the capacity to pay attention….Meditators become more relaxed the longer they have been at it. At the

same time they become more alert, something other ways to relax fail to bring about because they do not train the ability to pay attention.[15]

Indian spiritual teacher Swami Muktananda teaches, "Your daily needs are fulfilled with meditation, and meditation is also the place of rest from everyday life."[16] Sri Chinmoy, who worked with the United Nations on peace efforts, explains that "[m]editation is like going to the bottom of the sea where everything is calm and tranquil. On the surface of the sea there may be a multitude of waves, but the sea is not affected below."[17] After decades of research, Daniel Goleman and Richard Davidson find evidence that in training the brain through meditation, "An altered trait—a new characteristic that arises from a meditation practice—endures apart from meditation itself. Altered traits shape how we behave in our daily lives, not just during or immediately after we meditate."[18] Meditation has the ability to create lasting change in our brains and in our behavior. How we live our lives can be altered through the practice of regular meditation, which can enable us to live more mindfully. This supports the intermingled nature of meditation and mindfulness.

There Are Many Paths Up the Mountain

Before learning mindfulness techniques, I practiced a type of silent mantra meditation; the mantra is a Sanskrit word given to me by a trained meditation teacher and is repeated silently during the meditation practice. There are a number of similarities between mantra meditation and the formal technique of mindfulness meditation, including the concepts of connecting with the breath and becoming aware of the present moment. Additionally, the actual techniques are similar in terms of body posture on either a chair or cushion, length of time (typically 20–30 minutes), and the use of a support—which is the mantra in mantra meditation compared with the support of the breath or sound in mindfulness meditation. In comparing mindfulness meditation with mantra meditation:

Mindfulness meditation is commonly employed as a tool to gain insight into the nature of the mind and body, whereas the sound or mantra in mantra meditation is proposed to act as the most effective vehicle for directing and focusing the attention and awareness of the body and mind.[19]

In terms of mantra meditation, the mantra has been defined as "the purifier of the mind."[20] A mantra is a sacred word that embodies "a spiritually beneficial vibratory potency."[21] The mantra is repeated in rhythm with ingoing and outgoing breaths, which leads to a meditative state.[22] The mantra meditation I practice dates back about 5,000 years to ancient India, whereas the mindfulness meditation I learned in my Master of Science program has its roots in a Tibetan Buddhist tradition, dating back to around the 7th century CE.

The Fallacy of the New Age Label

Meditation is ancient. Nearly all cultures and religions, including Buddhism, Christianity, Judaism, and Islam, have evidence of their own form of meditation dating back thousands of years. In the past several decades, the focus on meditation in Western culture has taken on a more secular perspective and focuses more on the mental and physical health benefits of different meditation practices. The popularity of the term "mindfulness" has emerged from these secular practices. I believe this has led to the confusion between the terms "meditation" and "mindfulness." I think that to some people saying "mindfulness" makes the practice seem more secular and mainstream. Perhaps "mindfulness" seems more palatable for general audiences in corporate or educational settings. The reality is that meditation and authentic, *formal* mindfulness practices (e.g., mindfulness meditation) are equivalent in nature, even though there are many different forms of meditation techniques. In comparing meditation with *informal* mindfulness practices, I believe meditation and mindfulness are part and parcel of each other. They coexist. Meditating requires a certain level of being mindful, and mindfulness can grow through the regular practice of meditation.

My past studies and practices have been rooted in an Indian tradition, and the term "meditation" has always been used by my teachers, in books I've read, and in my training; therefore, I will be utilizing the term "meditation" throughout this book when discussing my formal practice of meditation. I will use the term "mindfulness" when I refer to informal practices. I will also use the term "mindful" when discussing the effects of meditation in daily life.

Notes

1. Mindfulness Association. (2021). What is mindfulness? Retrieved from https://www.mindfulnessassociation.net/what-is-mindfulness/
2. Miller, J. P. (2014). *The contemplative practitioner: Meditation in education and the workplace* (2nd ed.). Toronto: University of Toronto Press. p. 40.
3. Nairn, R. (2001). *Diamond mind: A psychology of meditation.* Boulder: Shambhala. p. 14.
4. Neff, K. (2011). *Self-compassion: The proven power of being kind to yourself.* New York: William Morrow/HarperCollins.
5. Kabat-Zinn, J. (1994). *Wherever you go there you are.* New York: Hachette. p. 4.
6. See Nairn, R. (2001). p. 14.
7. Williams, M., & Kabat-Zinn, J. (Eds.). (2013). *Mindfulness: Diverse perspectives on its meaning, origins and applications.* London: Routledge.
8. See Kabat-Zinn (1994). p. 4.
9. Hanson, R. & Mendius, R. (2009). *Buddha's brain: The practical neuroscience of happiness, love, and wisdom.* Oakland: New Harbinger Publications. p. 83.
10. See Nairn, R. (2001). p. 24.
11. Choden. (September 7, 2019). *Lecture: What is mindfulness?* Samye Ling Tibetan Centre: University of Aberdeen.
12. Germer, C. K. (2009). *The mindful path to self-compassion: Freeing yourself from destructive thoughts and emotions.* New York: The Guilford Press. p. 39.
13. Rinpoche, Y. M. (2007). *The joy of living: Unlocking the secret and science of happiness.* New York: Three Rivers Press. p. 43.

14 Dalai Lama, & Ed. Nicholas Vreeland. (2001). *An open heart: Practicing compassion in everyday life*. Boston: Little Brown and Company. p. 46.
15 Goleman, D. (1988). *The meditative mind: The varieties of meditative experiences*. New York: Putnam. pp. 166–168.
16 Muktananda, S. (1978). *Play of consciousness*. South Fallsburg, NY: Syda Foundation. p. 13.
17 Chinmoy, S. (1997). *The wings of joy*. New York: Fireside. p. 30.
18 Goleman, D. and Davidson, R. J. (2017). *Altered traits: Science reveals how meditation changes your mind, brain, and body*. New York: Avery. p. 6.
19 Lynch, J., Prihodova, L., Dunne, P. J., McMahon, G., Carroll, A., Walsh, C., & White, B. (2018). Impact of mantra meditation on health and well-being: A systematic review protocol. *European Journal of Integrative Medicine, 18*, 30–33. (Quote from p. 31). doi: https://doi.org/10.1016/j.eujim.2018.01.008
20 Yukteswar, S. (1990). *The holy science* (8th ed.). Los Angeles: Self-Realization Fellowship. p. 87.
21 Yogananda, P. (1993). *Autobiography of a yogi* (12th ed.). Los Angeles: Self-Realization Fellowship. p. 22.
22 Muktananda, S. (1978). *Play of consciousness*. South Fallsburg, NY: Syda Foundation.

2

Why Should We Care about the Well-Being of Teachers?

A New Beginning

People assume that I left teaching because I couldn't stand it anymore. Perhaps I grew tired of unrealistic teacher expectations, endless essays to grade, discipline problems, being bogged down with meaningless bureaucratic tasks, and the constant threat of school violence. Perhaps after over 20 years of teaching, I just became one of the many teachers who burned out, unable to make it to the finish line of retirement. These are all incorrect assumptions. Well, in a way, these are incorrect. I did experience these challenges as a teacher, but I was able to cope with these issues in a way that safeguarded me from the harmful effects and the burnout that they can lead to.

I loved teaching English. I'm a nerd. Teaching literature and helping students to develop their writing skills were exciting for me. I still miss it. However, I was drawn to another purpose. After witnessing so many of my colleagues and my students suffer from stress, anxiety, depression, and not feeling their best, I knew I had to share what helped to give me the edge mentally and physically: meditation. At the top of my game (and the pay scale), I defied logic and left my high school classroom to become a teacher on a larger scale.

Welcome to my new classroom. Our learning objective is to determine how meditation can help you cope with the struggles of life while enabling you to have the mental and physical edge to be healthier and happier.

The Significance of Teachers

Teachers are the most significant factor in the classroom. Period. This might seem like an obvious statement, but it cannot be said enough. Teachers are, in fact, the most important component in the entire education system. Above and beyond having the latest technology and newly renovated buildings, the actual teacher holds the most power to render the learning experience as beneficial and rewarding or meaningless and filled with strife. There are more and more requirements for continued education credits and in-house teacher development sessions. Ensuring that teachers are up to date on employing the best strategies for attaining academic standards is certainly essential. However, in tandem with bolstering teachers' pedagogical and content knowledge, there must be an equal emphasis placed upon the health and well-being of teachers, including the affective nature of teachers. The role of the teacher, including their personality and emotional state, is one of the most powerful factors in any classroom.

Take a moment and reflect upon your own experience as a student. Think about the teachers who had the most positive impact upon you. Think about the teachers you learned the most from. Think about the teachers who inspired you, who made you want to be the best version of yourself. How would you describe these teachers? How would you describe their personality? What was their emotional state like?

Now bring to mind a few teachers who caused you to dread going to a certain class. How were their personality, mood, and demeanor different from those of the teachers whom you connected with more positively?

Pause for a moment or two to reflect upon your experiences as a student and how you felt about different teachers and why.

Years ago, I was part of a consortium of teachers and administrators who were tasked to work with students from various high schools to determine how, according to students, we could best improve education for all learners. Many of the administrators I worked with assumed that students would be demanding better technology. However, students indicated that having a teacher who not only was competent but also demonstrated kindness and compassion and who made personal connections with students was the most important factor in their education.[1] I am reminded of the lesson imparted by renowned child psychologist Dr. Haim Ginott[2]:

> I have come to a frightening conclusion. I am the decisive element in the classroom. It is my personal approach that creates the climate. It is my daily mood that makes the weather. As a teacher I possess tremendous power to make a child's life miserable or joyous. I can be a tool of torture or an instrument of inspiration. I can humiliate or humor, hurt or heal. In all situations it is my response that decides whether a crisis will be escalated or de-escalated, and a child humanized or de-humanized.

Ginott's insight speaks to the significance of the classroom teacher. The teacher is not simply a repository of facts and figures, someone there to impart knowledge, to cover the curriculum, and to prepare students for passing standardized exams. Teachers lead by example. They set the tone for the classroom and often teach indirectly by means of their persona. Students who perceive their teacher as being more mindful may have an increased tendency to embody mindfulness, compassion, and self-compassion themselves.[3] Similarly, teachers' emotions play a crucial role in creating the classroom environment and determining students' emotional states.[4]

In conjunction with pedagogically preparing lessons and focusing on academic content, teachers should invest time in their own well-being because a teacher's emotional behavior can be more significant than instructional behavior, and there is an "emotional contagion" from teacher to students.[5] This theory of emotional contagion is further explored by a group of researchers who examined how teacher personality can affect teacher effectiveness in secondary mathematics and English teachers.[6] Findings suggest that teacher personality predicted teacher effectiveness in terms of teacher support and student performance self-efficacy (PSE) and indicate that teachers can spread both positive and negative emotions, most notably that "teacher neuroticism may affect students' PSE through the transmission of negative emotions via social modeling and emotion contagion, resulting in lower self-confidence among students."[7]

What does all of this mean? Simply that researchers are now discovering what students have anecdotally known for ages: A teacher has the power to make the learning environment enjoyable or dreadful, and indeed a teacher's state of being can affect the well-being of the students. So, yes, figuring out how to improve teacher well-being is pretty darn important. In fact, it needs to be a priority. We must empower teachers with efficacious tools for helping their well-being so, in turn, they can create a healthy environment of learning and growth for all. What is one of the best ways to do this? Meditation. The practice of meditation is scientifically proven to benefit both the body and the mind. Meditation is a deceptively simple yet powerful tool to help reduce the effects of stress while fostering healthier relationships with oneself and others.

Teaching and the Ego

When I taught undergraduate and graduate students studying to become teachers, I would tell them to take out a piece of paper and write really big, filling up the entire paper:

"NEVER TAKE ANYTHING PERSONALLY."

Then I advised them to put that paper somewhere they would see it on a regular basis—maybe their personal workspace or where they got ready in the morning. This was to become a sort of mantra for them as they completed their student teaching and as they entered the teaching profession. This isn't always easy to do, however. When a student screams obscenities at you and says they hate you and your class, well, it's difficult not to take that personally. A natural inclination might be to respond in like manner to the student. Or teachers may carry that feeling of failure, anger, or hopelessness with them throughout the rest of their day, week, year, or even career. However, as many veteran teachers have learned the hard way, student behavior often has more to do with the student's own fears, anxieties and/or personal struggles. Taking their behavior personally not only is usually harmful for the teacher but also can prevent or delay finding the appropriate help that the student needs.

By learning how to view classroom situations and student behavior more objectively, one finds that a shift occurs from being reactionary and taking offense to being more responsive and impartial. Meditation can help teachers have less egoic-based reactions and be more neutral and reflective when dealing with challenging situations. I always think of the story my father told me years ago about a prison warden he knew. The warden told him that one of the reasons people committed crimes that landed them in prison was that somebody had offended them and they just couldn't let it go. If left unchecked, the ego certainly has the ability to take over our behavior and lead to destructive outcomes. Now, this cautionary tale might seem rather extreme; however, it does shed light on the importance of recognizing one's own egoic-based reactions.

When we think of the ego, several ideas may come to mind. Perhaps we think back to our college psychology course and remember Freud's id, ego, and superego. In psychology, a basic definition of the ego is "A component of personality that seeks to gain pleasure; it operates on the reality principle where impulses are controlled when situations aren't favorable for meeting its demands."[8] Informally, we may think of someone who exudes too much confidence and appears to be pompous to be egotistical. However, the ego works in mysterious ways. The demure person who appears insecure and constantly puts themselves down might have just as large of an ego as the extrovert who boasts of their accomplishments. Basically, the ego perceives every person, interaction, and situation as either for or against "me."[9] Modern spiritual teacher Eckhart Tolle explains that the ego always feels under attack and "As long as the egoic mind is running your life, you cannot truly be at ease."[10] Egoic-based reactions make everything extremely personal, even when they really shouldn't be. Reacting through our ego can prevent us from objectively perceiving problems or situations, close us off from insights that can help us respond more harmoniously and with greater wisdom, and even escalate problems.

Of course, then there is the acknowledgement of students having their own egos and how their sense of feeling wronged or disrespected in some way might contribute to their behavior. We might see a student who feels disrespected by another student lash out, or we might see a student who feels slighted in some way just shut down or even stop coming to school. As teachers, we want to first acknowledge that students are struggling with their own sense of self and belonging and then acknowledge that the actual behavior we are witnessing in the moment may be the surface level of a much larger and more complex issue. Again, the key here is to "NEVER TAKE ANYTHING PERSONALLY." As teachers, we are held to higher standards than the typical person. We are tasked with the obligation to rise above the fray while we are dealing with difficult students and challenging classroom situations. This is not easy. In fact, it might seem that we need to attain sainthood status to achieve this. Believe me. I've taught students who threw things at me, who swore at me, and who made physical threats toward me. I'm not being dismissive or cavalier about aggressive student behavior or the increased numbers of students with mental health concerns. These are real issues, and teaching becomes increasingly more challenging each year because of them.

How Can Meditation Help?

How exactly can meditation help minimize egoic-based reactions as a teacher navigates a multitude of student egos? How can meditation help to support teacher overall health and well-being? Why should teachers (and administrators, support staff, or anybody involved with any aspect of education) practice meditation on a regular basis when they already have too much to do? I have spent several decades exploring these topics.

Essentially, meditation helps to ground us in the present moment and, in doing so, helps to lessen our tendency to ruminate on past issues or fret about the future. Being in the present moment enables us to become more aware of our egoic reactions. This awareness is the start of our becoming free of our own destructive ego. Meditation centers us, it helps to release stress from the mind and body, and it instills a sense of peace within and around us. Meditating creates a space around us and enables us to view a given situation from a different vantage point. We can begin to perceive what is taking place with greater clarity because we are now less emotional and have an increased ability to be more objective rather than responding through our ego.

This ties in with another key outcome of meditation: compassion. Meditation cultivates compassion for others and for oneself. Working with a more compassionate mindset for others and self leads to a sense of unity and awareness of the interconnectedness of all people in our own surroundings and around the world. The compassion that teachers model in the classroom is critical for teaching students to be more compassionate toward others and toward themselves. Having greater compassion for self and others reverberates out to the students and therefore not only will benefit teachers but can positively affect the ways that students perceive themselves and others. Think about the implications this could have on issues such as discrimination and bullying.

Meditation also fosters creativity and problem-solving skills. The best teachers embody a complementary blend of passion and compassion. Meditation enlivens the sense of newness, of enthusiasm, and of being able to perceive difficulties more as challenges and opportunities than as problems and defeats. Even mundane tasks can become more meaningful and exciting. Not only can the practice of meditation have a profound effect on issues such as burnout and teacher attrition, but meditation can promote greater clarity and can lead to insights and solutions to problems, enabling teachers to be highly competent.

A Matter of Urgency

There is a crisis in the American education system. As a matter of urgency, we need to address the high levels of stress and anxiety experienced by our teachers and our students. Greater focus needs to be placed on ways to help teachers cope with the challenges of teaching in today's climate of school violence and meeting the diverse needs of students who are struggling with mental health concerns. When I started teaching, there was a strong mindset that schools were solely for academic learning and that students should be learning about social and emotional behavior at home. Many of my colleagues early on didn't believe we had the obligation, or even the right, to be teaching about concepts related to social and emotional health and well-being. That was the job of the parents to teach about these concepts. Teachers were to teach their content area and stick to the curriculum with great fidelity.

I remember being hired to teach high school English and being handed the very prescribed, detailed curriculum for each course that dictated exactly what I was to teach each day. For example, a particular poem would be taught for precisely one and a half class periods. There was no room for deviation. There was little room for that teachable moment. There certainly was no room for peppering in a quick discussion on learning to be in the present moment or better understanding our emotional state. I remember being observed one day, and the principal questioning me about a particular non-fiction piece I was teaching. It was the same non-fiction article that was in the curriculum, but instead of using the original one that was over a decade old, I found an updated version of the same non-fiction selection that provided students with more contemporary examples they could relate to. I had to justify this slight change to the curriculum.

Then there were some of the older teachers in the department who would literally chase after any teacher who went "rogue" in any way. There was a teacher who frantically yelled my name down a crowded hallway as she ran after me. She caught up to me and, in a state of great panic, declared that she heard from a student that I allowed that student to include an introduction on his outline! *That was a violation!* Oh, the problems we thought we had in schools in the 1990s.

As I will discuss in Part II, the tragedy of the Columbine school shootings forever changed the face of education. That was the beginning of a shift that occurred not only in schools but in all areas of society. Decades later, we are forced to deal with the reality that addressing mental health and well-being must be a priority for schools. From the extreme cases of violence and hatred to the more subtle problems of anxieties and depression experienced by students and teachers, the need for teaching about and providing support for mental health is urgent. Deciding not to focus in a significant way on mental health and well-being, in the wake of everything being experienced in the world right now, is tantamount to deciding not to teach reading and math. And just as teachers need to be educated in the academic subject they teach, they must also be trained in techniques to improve one's mental health and well-being. *It begins with teachers.* The sooner teachers can get the help they need to support their own health and well-being, the sooner they can help their students address their mental health and well-being.

Teacher Burnout and Attrition

Why would anyone want to become a teacher? Long summer breaks are no longer good enough reasons, and it has become increasingly more difficult for the restorative effects of summers to carry teachers through an exhausting school year.

Within ten years of teaching, I became one of the senior members of my department of about 15 people. A significant number of teachers cycled through our department over the 23 years I was there; many left with less than ten years of experience, expressing that the level of stress was too much and/or that they wanted to find greener pastures. Stress and burnout have become almost synonymous with the teaching profession. In a cynical sense, one could say, "Who cares?" Teachers should just toughen up or move on to another profession. However, the retention of qualified teachers has become a serious issue. Teacher attrition poses a considerable problem that needs to be addressed and can be characterized as "good" teachers leaving the field for the "wrong reasons."[11] I saw firsthand the U.S. attrition rate of two thirds of teachers leaving the profession prior to retirement.[12] Multiple factors, including compensation, contribute to teacher attrition; however, working conditions and job dissatisfaction are two main reasons for teachers leaving.[13] The dire need for qualified teachers in certain content areas and in low-income schools has led the government to pay off student loans for teachers in these fields.[14] This issue of teacher attrition is further complicated by the decline of students majoring in education over the past several decades.[15]

In my experience as a teacher and as a department chair, I believe stress exacerbates the desire to leave teaching; therefore, the issue of teacher stress must be addressed. Can practices such as meditation benefit teachers in coping with stress and reducing burnout? In the past decade, there has been an upsurge of studies seeking to answer this question. From personal experience and from my research, I believe that practices such as meditation can absolutely provide teachers with an efficacious tool to survive and thrive in the classroom.

Please don't think that, by advocating practicing meditation for teachers, I'm being naïve or dismissive of some of the other larger issues present in the field of education, such as teacher compensation or workload. Teacher salaries need to be examined across the country and adjusted to be in alignment with other professionals. For example, when I had taught for over 15 years, had a doctorate, was the head of my department and making only in the $60K range, I had former students who just graduated from college making more money than I was. That being said, the top of the pay scale (for my district, a teacher hit the top of the pay scale after 19 years of teaching in the district) was around $100,000 at the time I left in 2020. Truthfully, I felt grateful to have that salary, but I know that not all teachers are compensated that well nationally, and I had to work for almost 20 years to reach that salary.

Other key issues facing teachers are the unrealistic workload and demands placed upon their time, which are exacerbated by large class sizes and inadequate support services for students. I am fully aware that these very real issues also factor into teacher well-being and problems with burnout and attrition. These points are not being debated. However, my intention is to provide insights, research, and a firsthand account of how meditation can be beneficial for one's overall health and well-being, which can support teachers, or anyone for that matter, professionally and personally.

Notes

1 S.H.A.S.D.A. (2005). *Student leadership forum*. Pittsburgh, PA: The South Hills Area School Districts Association.
2 Ginott, H. G. (1972). *Teacher & child: A book for parents and teachers*. New York: Collier. pp. 15–16.
3 Colaianne, B. A., Galla, B. M., & Roeser, R. W. (2020). Perceptions of mindful teaching are associated with longitudinal change in adolescents' mindfulness and compassion. *International Journal of Behavioral Development, 44*(1), 41–50. doi: 10.1177/0165025419870864.
4 Zarate, K., Maggin, D. M., & Passmore, A. (2019). Meta-analysis of mindfulness training on teacher well-being. *Psychology in the Schools, 56*(10), 1700–1715. doi: https://doi.org/10.1002/pits.22308.
5 Becker, E. S., Goetz, T., Morger, V., & Ranellucci, J. (2014). The importance of teachers' emotions and instructional behavior for their students' emotions – an experience sampling analysis. *Teaching and Teacher Education, 43*, 15–26. (Quote on p. 22). doi: https://doi.org/10.1016/j.tate.2014.05.002.
6 Kim, L. E., Dar-Nimrod, I., and MacCann, C. (2018). Teacher personality and teacher effectiveness in secondary school: Personality predicts teacher support and student self-efficacy but not academic achievement. *Journal of Educational Psychology, 110*(3), 309–323.
7 Ibid. p. 311.
8 Cherry, K. (2010). *Essentials of psychology: An introductory guide to the science of human behavior*. New York: Fall River Press. p. 252.
9 Klein, L. (2016). *TEDx talk, Meditation: Teaching from within* https://www.youtube.com/watch?v=o2JPumXZtlw.

10 Tolle, E. (1999). *The power of now: A guide to spiritual enlightenment.* Vancouver: Namaste Publishing. p. 46.
11 Kelchtermans, G. (2017). 'Should I stay or should I go?': Unpacking teacher attrition/retention as an educational issue. *Teachers and Teaching, 23*(8), 961–977. (Quote p. 965). doi:10.1080/13540602.2017.1379793.
12 Carver-Thomas, D., and Darling-Hammond, L. (2019). The trouble with teacher turnover: How teacher attrition affects students and schools. *Education Policy Analysis Archives, 27*(36), 1–32; Sutcher, L., Darling-Hammond, L., and Carver-Thomas, D. (2016). *A coming crisis in teaching? Teacher supply, demand, and shortages in the U.S.* (https://learningpolicyinstitute.org/product/coming-crisis-teaching). Palo Alto, CA: Learning Policy Institute.
13 Garcia, E., and Weiss, E. (2019). *U.S. schools struggle to hire and retain teachers.* (The Second Report in 'The Perfect Storm in the Teacher Labor Market' Series). Washington, DC: Economic Policy Institute. See also Sutcher, et al. (2016).
14 U.S. Department of Education. (2019). Student loans, forgiveness. Retrieved from https://www2.ed.gov/fund/grants-college.html?src=pn.
15 National Center for Education Statistics. (2019). Digest of education statistics. Retrieved from https://nces.ed.gov/programs/digest/d12/tables/dt12_310.asp. Passy, J. (2018). Fewer Americans are majoring in education, but will students pay the price? Retrieved from https://www.marketwatch.com/story/fewer-americans-are-majoring-in-education-but-will-students-pay-the-price-2018-02-14.

3

Effects of Meditation on the Body and Mind

Effects of Meditation on Physical Health and Well-Being

Suntan oil and lemon juice. In high school, my friends chased the deep, sun-kissed tan with sun/lemon highlighted hair. I even knew people who rubbed baby oil on themselves and sunbathed on black roofs to absorb as much of the sun as possible. Meanwhile, I was slathering myself in the highest level of SPF (sun protection factor) I could find and not because I burned easily. I had olive skin. If I wanted to, I could get a beautiful tan. But I was concerned about wrinkles. I was like 14. I was just a kid, and I was obsessed with staying young and being healthy. When I was 13, all I wanted was a subscription to *Prevention Magazine*. I have no idea how this started. My parents didn't have any of these concerns. Why am I bringing this up? Because from the time I was in my teens, I had a keen interest in finding out how to be healthy, have longevity, and look and feel my best—and I must add here—in a natural way. For decades, I have asked any person I've encountered who has lived a long and healthy life what their secret to longevity is. I have been fascinated in examining health and well-being since I was a teenager.

Then, in college, I was introduced to meditation at the age of 19. I met older, long-term meditators who seemed to have aged more gracefully than the typical person. They had a vibrancy, a youthfulness about them. Could this be the key ingredient I've been searching for? Now, at this point, there was little research available to me on the effects of meditation on health. I just intuitively sensed that these meditators were on to something. I've been meditating ever since.

Fast-forward several decades, and now there is a growing body of research that heralds the benefits of meditation for health and well-being. We can scientifically understand how exactly meditation can have an impact on our health. *(Full disclosure: Chapter 3 is a little heavy as I take you on a deeper dive into the various studies that document the scientific findings on how meditation impacts our minds and bodies.)*

One area that researchers have studied is the relationship between meditation and benefits to the immune system. In reviewing all relevant articles published between 1966—the publishing year of the first empirical paper on mindfulness meditation—and 2015, David S. Black and George M. Slavich narrowed their analysis down to the top 20 studies that met their criteria of being a randomized control trial of using mindfulness meditation as an intervention to evaluate immune function.[1] Their findings indicate that mindfulness meditation appears to be beneficial for reducing proinflammatory processes, improving immune function, and slowing cell aging.[2] Additionally, meditation can help to regulate the endocrine system, important for managing stress.[3] Threats—real or perceived—can interrupt homeostasis, increase heart rate and blood pressure, release hormones such as cortisol, and suppress systems such as the immune system while threat is perceived.[4] Meditation is linked with improved immune function, most notably with "immune cell stability, inflammation in response to stress, and responsiveness to a vaccine."[5]

Research also provides promising evidence of the positive effect of meditation on cardiovascular health. In a study comparing 115 meditating monks with 137 non-meditating monks and laymen, a group of researchers working out of Rajarata University of Sri Lanka found that the meditating monks presented higher HDL (high-density lipoprotein) cholesterol and lower overall cholesterol, suggesting a preventative effect on cardiovascular disease.[6] For cardiovascular patients, mindfulness-based interventions can improve their overall health and well-being in a number of ways, including reducing anxiety, depression, and systolic blood pressure.[7]

Another recent study looked at meditation and the effects on cardiovascular health in the U.S. by using the National Health Interview Survey of 61,267 participants and discovered that the 5,851 participants who reported practicing meditation had lower prevalences of hypercholesterolemia, diabetes, stroke, or coronary artery disease compared with the non-meditators surveyed.[8] This study, though promising in its overall link between meditation and cardiovascular health, does not factor in what types of meditation techniques were practiced or the length of time the participants practiced meditation. The factor of how long one has practiced meditation can be a significant aspect in the effects on one's health. As in any health program, the more consistent one is with the practice and the longer one practices, the more significant the results tend to be. Long-term meditation practice can yield cumulative results. Many studies look at short-term results and focus on the benefits of meditation after a shorter period of around eight weeks of practice. However, the long-term effects of meditation can be truly remarkable.

Effects of Meditation on the Brain and Mind

Not only is there a growing body of scientific research demonstrating the effects of meditation on physical health, there is also mounting support for the influence that meditation can have on one's mood, emotions, and cognition.[9] There is even the potential to rewire the brain through the practice of meditation. This idea of neuroplasticity offers promising hope for self-improvement. For example, Jon Kabat-Zinn discusses a study that he conducted with Richard Davidson in 2003 in which participants from a biotechnology company were divided into groups after initial baseline tests were conducted using electroencephalograms (EEGs).[10] One group participated in an 8-week Mindfulness-Based Stress

Reduction (MBSR) training; the other group was wait-listed. One aim of the study was to determine if practicing MBSR had any effect on the frontal and prefrontal cortex of the brain. The left prefrontal cortex is associated with positive emotions such as joy, happiness, and alertness, while the right prefrontal cortex is associated with emotions such as fear and sadness; previously, it was believed that these "temperamental set points" were "fixed for life."[11] Baseline tests showed similar patterns in the two groups; however, follow-up tests after 8 weeks of mindfulness showed that the meditators presented a "significant shift to a higher ratio of left-compared to right-sided activation."[12] Mindfulness caused a shift to "more positive emotion and more effective processing of difficult emotions while under stress."[13]

The scientific proof that we can take control of not only how we *feel* but how our brains are *wired* is lifechanging. Neuropsychologist Rick Hanson and neurologist Richard Mendius believe that because the mind is the origin of much of our suffering—ruminating on the past, fretting about the future—it can also be the cure of much of our suffering.[14] According to Choden and Heather Regan-Addis, two of the founders of the Mindfulness Association in the U.K., humans, through our evolutionary development, have been conditioned to gravitate to more of a threat mindset, but by applying the idea of "energy follows focus," we can choose to focus on more positive experiences such as kindness.[15] Hanson and Mendius believe that through this "*active* effort to internalize positive experiences... you're actually righting the neurological imbalance."[16] Not only can our thoughts build new neural structures, but practices such as mindfulness meditation can increase the gray matter—the cortical thickness of the brain in the key areas governing attention and compassion.[17] As humans, we have the power to actively improve our brains. Can there be a more compelling argument for meditating?

Although there is a proliferation of research noting the impact of meditation on the brain, it's critical to be cautious of just blindly accepting claims of meditation being a cure-all. Meditation is certainly not a panacea that can prevent and cure all ills of the body and mind. Daniel Goleman and Richard

Davidson, groundbreaking researchers linking the practice of meditation with neuroscience, discuss the promising effects that meditation could have on the brain and body; however, they warn that careful attention must be taken to consider things such as the type of meditation technique being studied since there are vastly different types of meditation and not all forms may indicate the same results.[18] Moreover, there could be a "Hawthorne effect," in which any positive change, not necessarily meditation, could lead to positive benefits being reported; this can especially be the case in beginning meditators who might simply be enthusiastic and "have positive hopes and expectations."[19] Meditation may be helpful for mental health, emotion regulation, and prevention of depression relapse, anxiety, and addiction disorders, but it's important to recognize that meditation can carry the risk of triggering past trauma, although instances of triggering were rare in an 8-week mindfulness course.[20] This is one of the reasons why having a trained meditation teacher is so important, and if you are under the care of a psychiatrist or therapist, you should discuss learning mindfulness techniques or meditation with your health-care provider prior to starting any mindfulness or meditation program.

Long-Term Effects of Meditation on Health and Aging

Many studies have examined the effects of short-term meditation interventions, such as the impact of 8-week mindfulness meditation programs on mental and physical health. Instinctually, one may assume that the longer one practices meditation, the more profound the changes/outcomes will be. But is this true? Are there any significant manifestations in long-term meditators compared with short-term or novice meditators? *Yes*.

Evidence in support of the supposition that there are significant effects experienced by long-term meditators is provided in a number of scientific studies, including research that examines the influence of meditation on epigenetics and how one biologically ages. According to the Centers for Disease Control and Prevention, "Epigenetics is the study of how your behaviors and environment can cause changes that affect the way your genes work."[21] Can the behavior of meditating cause beneficial epigenetic changes? The research in this field is fairly new; however, some promising results have appeared in studies linking long-term meditation with beneficial epigenetic influence.

In one such study, using blood samples of long-term meditators, who have been practicing meditation for at least 5 years, researchers have found that regular, long-term meditation practice can slow the epigenetic clock, indicating a preventive approach to age-related diseases.[22] More specifically, in long-term meditators over the age of 52, the rate of epigenetic aging decreased significantly, thereby suggesting that "the protective effect of meditation on epigenetic age acceleration may be progressive and cumulative."[23] Similarly, a study also analyzing blood samples from long-term meditators, who have been practicing Open-Monitoring meditation for at least 10 years, found that long-term meditation practice may have a positive impact on the molecular level of "particular health conditions, including neurological and psychiatric disorders, cardiovascular diseases, and cancer."[24]

Another promising area of research is the connection between long-term meditation practice and telomere length. In their groundbreaking book *The Telomere Effect*, Nobel Prize winner Elizabeth Blackburn and Elissa Epel explain that telomeres, located at the ends of chromosomes, play a significant role in how one ages.[25] "Telomeres are DNA-protein complexes that protect the end of linear chromosomes from degradation, fusion, or DNA repair processes."[26] Shorter telomeres are associated with premature aging and increased health risks, whereas longer telomeres are associated with a slowing of the aging process and a longer "healthspan—the number of years of our healthy life."[27] Practices such as meditation have been shown to lengthen telomeres and have a positive impact on health and aging.[28] However, "the effects of meditation on telomere length may be dose dependent and may take time to unfold," indicating that the longer one has practiced meditation, the greater the effects.[29]

A randomized control trial of 158 participants assigned to either an 8-week MBSR course or the control (Music Therapy Stress Reduction) group intervention found no significant change in telomere length in either group within the 8-week time frame, suggesting that changes to telomere length require more-intensive, long-term meditation practice.[30] A study utilizing blood samples to examine telomere lengths of long-term meditators compared with a control group discovered that while the control group showed age-related telomere changes, the long-term meditation group (having practiced meditation for at least 10 years) did not show these age-related effects to telomere length.[31] Anecdotally, I have witnessed long-term meditators who have slowed the aging clock, and personally, I believe that meditation is the closest thing we can get to a fountain of youth.

Long-Term Effects of Meditation on the Brain and Mind

By now, it's becoming clear that meditation can positively affect one's physical and mental health, but interestingly, it can also affect the way one is perceived by others. For example, in a study of long-term meditators and a control group, objective observers viewing still photographs perceived long-term meditators as being less neurotic and more mindful than short-term meditators, and long-term meditation practice may be linked to "observable differences in facial behavior."[32] Meditation, especially long-term practice, helps to instill a sense of calm, of enthusiasm, of happiness, of compassion, and of kindness. These qualities are not felt just by the meditator. Meditators carry these qualities with them into their daily activities, which can reverberate out to their surroundings and to those with whom they come into contact.

Long-term meditation can make one feel better and be perceived in a more positive manner, and this could be connected to actual structural changes that occur in the brain. Long-term meditation practice has been linked with neuroplastic changes in the brain and with having positive effects on the cortical thickness of the brain.[33] Investigating the impact of long-term loving kindness meditation, a study found increased cortical thickness in long-term meditators compared with a similar non-meditation control group, specifically in the left ventrolateral prefrontal cortex and anterior insula and "might thus be playing a key role in orchestrating generation of positive emotional states associated with loving-kindness meditation."[34]

Furthermore, the usual age-related shrinkage of the brain is lessened in meditators, and "for every year beyond fifty, the brains of practitioners were younger than their peers' by one month and twenty-two days."[35] Not only has regular practice of meditation been linked with increased gray matter of the brain, there is also evidence that it can positively affect the white matter of the brain. Whereas gray matter comprises the outer layer of the brain, white matter serves as the connector between different brain regions carrying impulses which affect various brain functions, including cognition.[36] Examining the effects of mindfulness meditation on white matter, researchers compared samples of long-term meditators (at least 5 years of practice) with matched non-meditators using magnetic resonance imaging (MRI) scans, and results indicate that the meditators did not show the normal age-related decline in white matter.[37]

Long-term meditation practice can affect the actual structure of the brain and may also affect our mental states and how we react to experiences. Goleman explains that "a meditator handles stress in a way that breaks up the threat-arousal-threat spiral. The meditator relaxes after a challenge passes more often than the nonmeditator...He perceives threat more accurately, and reacts with arousal only when necessary."[38] Similarly, Hanson and Mendius discuss the importance of the parasympathetic nervous system (PNS) for balancing out stress/threat modes; the PNS can be activated by regular meditation and can instill a sense of well-being.[39]

Some may argue that perhaps people who are drawn to meditation are already intrinsically happier, calmer, and naturally able to deal with stress before they even learn. This argument, however, is refuted by Cliff Saron, who conducted a longitudinal study comparing participants in a three-month retreat with a control group and used follow-up measures five months after the retreat.[40] Findings indicated that the effects of long-term meditation on emotion regulation, anxiety, and well-being may extend beyond correlation: "And the study dispels doubts that all the positive traits found in long-term meditators are simply due to self-selection, where people who already had those traits choose the practice or stay with it in the long run."[41]

Long-Term Meditation and Higher Levels of Being/Awareness

Can long-term meditation lead to higher levels of being and a different way of perceiving the world? Goleman and Davidson explain how regular meditation practice can create enduring altered traits, including "selflessness, equanimity, a loving presence, and impartial compassion" and lead to "a transformation that dramatically ups the limits on psychological science's ideas of human possibility."[42] Comparing advanced meditators to a form of superheroes, Patrick Jones, a researcher in the fields of psychology and spirituality, explains that "there is a growing literature documenting significant differences between beginners and advanced mindfulness practitioners (long term meditators) who may be using the same 'methods' but attaining very different 'states.'"[43] These states include resistance to disease, slowing of the aging process, improved cognitive function, enhanced resilience, fearlessness, selflessness, and heightened powers such as clairaudience, telepathy, and clairvoyance.[44] Caroline Myss, who is a medical intuitive, has worked with doctors and patients to understand how illnesses can be linked with one's emotional and psychological states. She explains that people can heal themselves through tapping into their energy and offers a meditation to heal and awaken the seven chakras of the body, so that the meditator is able to evolve into higher states of consciousness.[45] The belief in higher states of being or consciousness can be seen in both spiritual and psychological realms.

Examining the lived experience of long-term meditators, a group of researchers applied an interpretative phenomenological process and interviewed six women who practiced daily meditation for more than ten years.[46] Emergent themes included "cultivation of self-awareness," "increased equanimity, compassion, acceptance of self and others," "transcendent, peak experiences," "cultivation and deepening of personal spirituality," and "life purpose and meaning."[47] In terms of transcendent, peak experiences, the participants described feelings of oneness with something larger than themselves, an awakening of their senses, a sense of profound joy and peace, feelings of floating, and an awareness of the "expansiveness of the universe."[48] These practitioners didn't always experience these sensations, and each participant practiced different forms of meditation—three types of which didn't teach the idea of transcendent or peak experiences; these occurrences emerged on their own without any preconceived notion of them.[49]

Creativity Linked to Meditation

These higher states are referred to in various ways, including *self-actualization*, which is defined by pioneer of humanistic psychology Abraham Maslow as "The full use and exploitation of talents, capacities, potentialities."[50] One of the facets of self-actualization is creativity, in which Maslow clarifies his notion of "self-actualized creativeness" as including "a certain kind of humor, a tendency to do *anything* creatively: for instance, teaching and so forth."[51] The idea of creativity being an outcome of meditation is supported by Indian philosopher and spiritual leader Osho, who believes "Meditation is creativity" and, in dissolving the ego through meditation, a person becomes creative in their own individual ways, regardless of one's profession or endeavors.[52] In his book *The 7 Habits of Highly Effective People: Powerful Lessons in Personal Change*, Stephen Covey advises readers to take time out to "sharpen the saw" through practices such as meditation to improve performance and be most effective.[53]

Further evidence connecting meditation and creativity is found in a thematic review of various studies, which arrives at the conclusion that there is a definite connection between meditation and creativity in the field of education.[54] Ultimately, the idea of meditation fostering creativity makes sense, and according to Carl Rogers, renowned psychologist and one of the founders of humanistic psychology, creativity cannot be forced: it must be allowed to emerge, and a human's tendency is to "become his potentialities" which "awaits only the proper conditions to be released and expressed."[55] Meditation helps to create these conditions by centering the practitioner in the present moment and instilling a sense of calm, clarity, and openness that allows creative insights to emerge.

Other studies also link meditation with creativity, indicating that formal meditation techniques can have a positive effect on creativity. For example, one such study found that both mindfulness meditation and concentrative meditation increased creative performance.[56] A different research study conducted an eight-week, pre-post-test analysis of a group of participants who attended a weekly mindfulness meditation course and a control group of participants attending a weekly leadership class.[57] Survey questions for pre-post-tests focused on qualities considered important for successful leadership, including creativity. Findings were promising for suggesting the connection between mindfulness meditation and creativity; the researchers stated that "the most compelling findings of this study was that regular mindfulness practice resulted in greater promotional regulatory focus or propensity for turning creative ideas into reality."[58]

It's important to note, however, that consistency and duration of meditation practice are key. The longer one practices meditation on a regular basis, the greater the effects of meditation on creativity will be. For example, a two-week study found no significant effects between meditation and creativity in participants who meditated and the active and control groups.[59] From my perspective, two weeks is not enough time to see significant impact from meditation. Most research examines an intervention period of at least eight weeks, and long-term meditation practice tends to yield more significant results.

Synchronicity Linked to Meditation

In regard to higher levels of awareness, there is the phenomenon in transpersonal psychology called "synchronicity" that was coined by Carl Jung. According to Jung, the term synchronicity refers to "a coincidence in time of two or more causally unrelated events which have the same or a similar meaning."[60] Synchronicity is the occurrence of meaningful coincidences that create "an insight into an order of existence that integrates the personal and mundane with the universal and eternal," and the experience gives rise to a feeling of a deep connection between the individual and the universe.[61] Jung clarifies, "What I found were 'coincidences' which were connected so meaningfully that their 'chance' concurrence would represent a degree of improbability."[62] Deepak Chopra explains that one of the best ways to prime oneself for being open to experiences of synchronicity is to practice meditation—ideally twice a day for 15 to 20 minutes each time.[63] Bethany Butzer, a researcher in the field of positive and transpersonal psychology, agrees that meditation can be the conduit through which synchronicity occurs.[64]

Further supporting meditation's connection with synchronicity, Gabriel Crane explains that the experience of synchronicity is invoked by becoming calm and in the present moment, which can occur through practices such as meditation.[65] In fact, synchronicity can "enhance productivity and creativity" and "may not be 'one-off' events but rather doorways that lead us into a version of reality where everything is meaningfully and acausally connected."[66] For educators, the concept of synchronicity is promising because experiences of synchronicity can lead to increased teachable moments.[67]

In my personal and professional experience, I believe that the practice of meditation has enabled me to encounter increased moments of synchronicity. Meditation not only creates the conditions for synchronicity to arise but also enables one to be more open to and aware of such moments.

Bottom Line

What I have discovered through my research on meditation and through my own experience is that meditation is one of the best things you can do to benefit your overall health and well-being. It's both cost-effective and natural. Once you learn to meditate, it's free. I cannot say enough about how good meditating is for your health, *but* the teacher in me has to give the CYA (cover your ass) disclaimer: Meditation does not replace medical care; meditation is intended to be an enhancement, an additional tool to use in conjunction with one's regular health-care practice and medical doctors. Nevertheless, for most people, there are no harmful side effects, and in my experience, meditating opens one up to healing on all levels. It enables one to have greater overall awareness of their mind and body in order to be more in tune with what their body and mind need. If practiced consistently, meditation helps to create more balance and harmony in the mind and body and can have profound effects on how one looks, feels, and functions.

Notes

1 Black, D. S., & Slavich, G. M. (2016). Mindfulness meditation and the immune system: A systematic review of randomized controlled trials. *Annals of the New York Academy of Sciences*, *1373*(1), 13–24. https://doi.org/10.1111/nyas.12998.
2 Ibid.
3 Pascoe, M. C., Thompson, D. R., & Ski, C. F. (2020). Meditation and endocrine health and wellbeing. *Trends in Endocrinology & Metabolism*, *31*(7), 469–477. https://doi.org/10.1016/j.tem.2020.01.012.
4 Ibid.
5 Kok, B. E., Waugh, C. E., & Fredrickson, B. L. (2013). Meditation and health: The search for mechanisms of action. *Social and Personality Psychology Compass, 7*(1), 27–39. (Quote p. 29). https://doi.org/10.1111/spc3.12006.
6 Kumbukgolla, W., Jayaweera, J. A. A. S., Perera, P., & Hale, S. (2019). Detection of serum high-density lipoprotein cholesterol high levels in monks practicing samatha and vipassana meditation. *European Journal of Integrative Medicine*, *28*, 47–51. https://doi.org/10.1016/j.eujim.2019.05.005
7 Marino, F., Failla, C., Carrozza, C., Ciminata, M., Chilà, P., Minutoli, R., … Pioggia, G. (2021). Mindfulness-based interventions for physical and psychological wellbeing in cardiovascular diseases: A systematic review and meta-analysis. *Brain Sciences, 11*(6) http://dx.doi.org/10.3390/brainsci11060727
8 Krittanawong, C., Kumar, A., Wang, Z., Narasimhan, B., Jneid, H., Virani, S. S., & Levine, G. N. (2020). Meditation and cardiovascular health in the US. *The American Journal of Cardiology, 131*, 23–26. https://doi.org/10.1016/j.amjcard.2020.06.043

9 Marciniak, R., Sheardova, K., Cermáková, P., Hudeček, D., Sumec, R., & Hort, J. (2014). Effect of meditation on cognitive functions in context of aging and neurodegenerative diseases. *Frontiers in Behavioral Neuroscience, 8*, 17. http://dx.doi.org/10.3389/fnbeh.2014.00017; Goldstein, E., Topitzes, J., Brown, R. L., & Barrett, B. (2020). Mediational pathways of meditation and exercise on mental health and perceived stress: A randomized controlled trial. *Journal of Health Psychology, 25*(12), 1816–1830. https://doi.org/10.1177/1359105318772608; Sevinc, G., Rusche, J., Wong, B., Datta, T., Kaufman, R., Gutz, S. E., … Lazar, S. W. (2021). Mindfulness training improves cognition and strengthens intrinsic connectivity between the hippocampus and posteromedial cortex in healthy older adults. *Frontiers in Aging Neuroscience, 13*, 702796. http://doi.org/10.3389/fnagi.2021.702796; Zollars, I., Poirier, T. I., & Pailden, J. (2019). Effects of mindfulness meditation on mindfulness, mental well-being, and perceived stress. *Currents in Pharmacy Teaching and Learning, 11*(10), 1022–1028. https://doi.org/10.1016/j.cptl.2019.06.005
10 Kabat-Zinn, J. (2018). A study in happiness--meditation, the brain, and the immune system. *Mindfulness, 9*, 1664–1667.
11 Ibid. p. 1665.
12 Ibid. p. 1666.
13 Ibid. p. 1666.
14 Hanson, R., & Mendius, R. (2009). *Buddha's brain: The practical neuroscience of happiness, love, and wisdom*. Oakland, USA: New Harbinger Publications.
15 Choden, & Regan-Addis, H. (2018). *Mindfulness based living course*. Winchester: O Books. p. 44.
16 See Hanson and Mendius (2009). p. 75.
17 See Hanson and Mendius (2009); Hanson, R. (2013). *Hardwiring happiness: The new brain science of contentment, calm, and confidence*. New York: Harmony Books.
18 Goleman, D. and Davidson, R.J. (2017). *Altered traits: Science reveals how meditation changes your mind, brain, and body*. New York: Avery.
19 Ibid. pp. 72–73.
20 Creswell, J. D. (2017). Mindfulness interventions. *Annual Review of Psychology, 68*(1), 491–516. https://doi.org/10.1146/annurev-psych-042716-051139
21 Centers for Disease Control and Prevention. (2020). What is epigenetics? Retrieved from https://www.cdc.gov/genomics/disease/epigenetics.htm

22 Chaix, R., Alvarez-López, M. J., Fagny, M., Lemee, L., Regnault, B., Davidson, R. J., ... Kaliman, P. (2017). Epigenetic clock analysis in long-term meditators. *Psychoneuroendocrinology*, *85*, 210–214. https://doi.org/10.1016/j.psyneuen.2017.08.016
23 Ibid. p. 212.
24 García-Campayo, J., Puebla-Guedea, M., Labarga, A., Urdanoz, A., Roldan, M., Pulido, L., & Mendioroz, M. (2018). Epigenetic response to mindfulness in peripheral blood leukocytes involves genes linked to common human diseases. *Mindfulness*, *9*, 1146–1159.
25 Blackburn, E., & Epel, E. (2017). *The telomere effect*. New York: Grand Central Publishing.
26 Mendioroz, M., Puebla-Guedea, M., Montero-Marin, J., Urdanoz-Casado, A., Blanco-Luquin, I., Roldan, M., Labarga, A., & Garcia-Campayo, J. (2020). Telomere length correlates with subtelomeric DNA methylation in long-term mindfulness practitioners. *Scientific Reports*, *10*(4564), p. 1.
27 See Blackburn and Epel. (2017). p. 3.
28 Blackburn, E., & Epel, E. (2017). *The telomere effect*. New York: Grand Central Publishing; Schutte, N. S., Malouff, J. M., & Keng, S. (2020). Meditation and telomere length: A meta-analysis. *Psychol.Health*, *35*(8), 901–915. https://doi.org/10.1080/08870446.2019.1707827; Mendioroz, M., Puebla-Guedea, M., Montero-Marin, J., Urdanoz-Casado, A., Blanco-Luquin, I., Roldan, M., Labarga, A., & Garcia-Campayo, J. (2020). Telomere length correlates with subtelomeric DNA methylation in long-term mindfulness practioners. *Scientific Reports*, *10*(4564); Alda, M., Puebla-Guedea, M., Rodero, B., Demarzo, M., Montero-Marin, J., Roca, M., & Garcia-Campayo, J. (2016). Zen meditation, length of telomeres, and the role of experiential avoidance and compassion. *Mindfulness*, *7*, 651–659.
29 See Schutte et al. (2020). p. 910.
30 Keng, S., Looi, P. S., Tan, E. L. Y., Yim, O., Lai, P. S., Chew, S. H., & Ebstein, R. P. (2020). Effects of mindfulness-based stress reduction on psychological symptoms and telomere length: A randomized active-controlled trial. *Behavior Therapy*, *51*(6), 984–996. https://doi.org/10.1016/j.beth.2020.01.005
31 See Mendioroz et al. (2020).
32 Goldberg, S. B., Hirshberg, M., Tello, L. Y., Weng, H. Y., Flook, L., & Davidson, R. J. (2019). Still facial photographs of long-term meditators

are perceived by naïve observers as less neurotic, more conscientious and more mindful than non-meditating controls. p.1. *PloS One, 14*(8), e0221782. http://dx.doi.org/10.1371/journal.pone.0221782

33 Guidotti, R., Del Gratta, C., Perrucci, M. G., Romani, G. L., & Raffone, A. (2021). Neuroplasticity within and between functional brain networks in mental training based on long-term meditation. *Brain Sciences, 11*(8). http://dx.doi.org/10.3390/brainsci11081086

34 Engen, H. G., Bernhardt, B. C., Skottnik, L., Ricard, M., & Singer, T. (2018). Structural changes in socio-affective networks: Multi-modal MRI findings in long-term meditation practitioners. *Neuropsychologia, 116,* 26–33. p. 31. https://doi.org/10.1016/j.neuropsychologia.2017.08.024

35 See Goleman and Davidson (2017). p. 180.

36 Fields, R. D. (2022). Change in the brain's white matter: The role of the brain's white matter in active learning and memory may be underestimated. Retrieved from https://www.ncbi.nlm.nih.gov/pmc/articles/PMC3201847/

37 Laneri, D., Schuster, V., Dietsche, B., Jansen, A., Ott, U., & Sommer, J. (2016). Effects of long-term mindfulness meditation on brain's white matter microstructure and its aging. *Frontiers in Aging Neuroscience,* n/a. http://dx.doi.org/10.3389/fnagi.2015.00254

38 Goleman, D. (1988). *The meditative mind: The varieties of meditative experiences.* New York: Putnam. p. 165.

39 See Hanson and Mendius (2009).

40 See Goleman and Davidson (2017).

41 See Goleman and Davidson (2017). p. 95.

42 See Goleman and Davidson (2017). pp. 7–8.

43 Jones, P. (2019). Mindfulness training: Can it create superheroes? *Frontiers in Psychology, 10,* 1–13. (Quote from p. 3).

44 Ibid.

45 Myss, C. (1996). *Anatomy of the spirit: The seven stages of power and healing.* New York: Three Rivers Press.

46 Shaner, L., Kelly, L., Rockwell, D., & Curtis, D. (2017). Calm abiding: The lived experience of the practice of long-term meditation. *Journal of Humanistic Psychology, 57*(1), 98–121. https://doi.org/10.1177/0022167815594556

47 Ibid. pp. 105–111.

48 Ibid. p. 109.

49 Ibid.

50 Maslow, A. H. (1987). *Motivation and personality* (3rd ed.). New York: Addison, Wesley, Longman. p. 126.
51 Ibid. p. 160.
52 Osho. (1999). *Creativity: Unleashing the forces within*. New York: St. Martin's Griffin. p. 37.
53 Covey, S. R. (1990). *The 7 habits of highly effective people: Powerful lessons in personal change*. New York: Fireside/Simon and Schuster.
54 Henriksen, D., Richardson, C., & Shack, K. (2020). Mindfulness and creativity: Implications for thinking and learning. *Thinking Skills and Creativity, 37*, 100689. https://doi.org/10.1016/j.tsc.2020.100689
55 Rogers, C. R. (1989). *On becoming a person: A therapist's view of psychotherapy*. New York: Houghton Mifflin. p. 351.
56 Müller, B. C. N., Gerasimova, A., & Ritter, S. M. (2016). Concentrative meditation influences creativity by increasing cognitive flexibility. *Psychology of Aesthetics, Creativity, and the Arts, 10*(3), 278–286. https://doi.org/10.1037/a0040335
57 Brendel, W., Hankerson, S., Byun, S., & Cunningham, B. (2016). Cultivating leadership dharma: Measuring the impact of regular mindfulness practice on creativity, resilience, tolerance for ambiguity, anxiety and stress. *Journal of Management Development, 35*(8), 1056–1078. https://doi.org/10.1108/JMD-09-2015-0127
58 Ibid. p. 1067.
59 Bashmakova, I., & Shcherbakova, O. (2021). Just open your mind? A randomized, controlled study on the effects of meditation on creativity. *Frontiers in Psychology, 12* https://doi.org/10.3389/fpsyg.2021.663881
60 Jung, C. G. (2010). *Synchronicity: An acausal connecting principle*. Princeton: Princeton University Press. p. 25.
61 Hocoy, D. (2012). Sixty years later: The enduring allure of synchronicity. *Journal of Humanistic Psychology, 52*(4), 467–478. https://doi.org/10.1177/0022167812436427. p. 471.
62 See Jung. (2010). p. 21.
63 Chopra, D. (2003). *The spontaneous fulfillment of desire: Harnessing the infinite power of coincidence*. New York: Three Rivers Press.
64 Butzer, B. (2021). Does synchronicity point us towards the fundamental nature of consciousness? An exploration of psychology, ontology, and research prospects. *Journal of Consciousness Studies, 28*(3–4), 29–54.

65 Crane, G.S. (2018). Can synchronicity be invoked? Synchronistic inquiry and the nature of meaning. *Journal of Conscious Evolution*, *13*(13), article 3. https://digitalcommons.ciis.edu/vol13/iss13/3
66 Ibid. p. 11.
67 White, S.R. and Maycock, G.A. (2012). College teaching and synchronicity: Exploring the other side of teachable moments. *Community College Journal of Research and Practice*, *36*(5), 321–329. https://doi.org/10.1080/03601277.2010.500595

4

The Effects of Meditation on Teachers

"Leave Me Alone and Just Let Me Teach"

Let me set the scene. It's the end of summer, teachers are getting anxious for the new school year. What will their students be like this year? How will they adjust to their new schedule? Will they be able to stay a lesson ahead of the students with the new courses they're teaching? Will their observing principal be reasonable? Will the books they ordered be in on time? Will they be safe?

Now, pan to an auditorium filled with teachers there for the opening in-service session, professional development session, teacher training session—whatever you call them, these sessions are often viewed by teachers as pointless, annoying, time-filling meetings and activities that prevent them from having time to do the actual work they need to accomplish.

After sitting through over two decades of these sessions, I can tell you that teachers can be quite jaded about them. I was frequently one of these teachers. These sessions can create a feeling either of dread, anxiety, and panic about having another task—yet another new way to do something, another thing that administration will be critiquing in our lesson plans and in observations—or of meaninglessness that cause teachers to "check out" of the session.

With so many programs and in-service training sessions for teachers to improve their game (insert eyeroll), do we really need another program or practice for teachers? Teachers are already too busy and are thinking, "Just let us get out of this training session and go work in our rooms because there is sooooooo much to be done!!!"

When I had the opportunity to conduct professional development sessions for K-12 teachers and staff in our district on mindfulness and meditation, I was at first apprehensive, but I decided to present the sessions because they were made available to teachers and staff on a purely optional basis, in which teachers and support staff could choose my session on mindfulness and meditation or other types of professional development sessions. This is central to my philosophy on meditation and mindfulness. It should never be forced upon anyone. I believe that it's important for all faculty and staff (or students when pertaining to a young adult mindfulness program) to all be introduced to mindfulness/meditation in order to understand what it is and how it might benefit them, but then the decision to actually learn meditation needs to be determined by the individual.

Why should teachers, who are already inundated with teacher training programs and an overwhelming workload, bother with learning and practicing meditation? The answer: Meditation will not only help teachers to cope, it will give them an edge to be at the top of their game. Professionally and personally, teachers who meditate will reap the benefits mentally, physically, and in their interactions with others. A great deal of research has emerged in the last 15 years to support the argument that meditation is an effective practice to help reduce anxiety, stress, and burnout while increasing compassion, empathy, creativity, and positivity in classroom teachers.

The Link Between Meditation and Self-Actualization in Teachers

In 2008, I completed my doctoral degree, and my research was one of the few studies done on the effects of long-term meditation practice on classroom teachers. In fact, in the years leading up to writing my dissertation, when I was compiling my review of previous research studies, I had a difficult time finding much of anything on the topic. I considered switching my topic to something that was easier and more mainstream, but from my own experiences, I knew that this topic was extremely important to explore. I held to my convictions, and against any sort of logic, I decided to research the effects of meditation with a link to qualities of self-actualization in classroom teachers. Right. Somehow, I found a way to create an even more esoteric topic: I added the idea of self-actualization to meditation. In my own meditation practice, I felt that I had experienced qualities of self-actualization, and the more I meditated, the more I felt an increase in certain qualities of self-actualization, including creativity, spontaneity, compassion, acceptance, enthusiasm, sense of purpose, awareness of my own ego, and ability to perceive situations more accurately and objectively. Moving toward a state of self-actualization gave me an edge as a teacher, enabling me to be more in tune with my students while being more innovative, less reactive, and happier.

I wanted to see if other teachers who meditated experienced qualities of self-actualization. I interviewed and analyzed personal narratives of teachers (ranging from elementary to secondary teachers) who had practiced meditation for at least five years, and a definite link was found between meditation and qualities of self-actualization in these teachers. This study did not attempt to prove a full self-actualized state in teachers but rather determine if long-term meditating teachers experience qualities of self-actualization. As educators, we learn about the importance of each level of need being met for our students in order for them to learn and develop. Self-actualization is a higher state of awareness, and those who attain this state function on a higher level than the typical human, thus having an edge in their professional and personal lives. Self-actualized individuals can experience an increase in mental clarity and overall sense of well-being. According to Abraham Maslow,[1] qualities of self-actualization include

- ◆ Perception of reality
- ◆ Acceptance

- Spontaneity
- Being problem-centered (rather than ego-centered)
- Enjoying solitude
- Autonomy
- Fresh appreciation of even regular, daily activities
- Peak experiences (transcending oneself and having "intense concentration, intense sensuous experience, or self-forgetful and intense enjoyment of music or art"[2])
- Human kinship—"identification, sympathy, and affection for human beings in general…a genuine desire to help the human race"[3]
- Humility and respect
- Interpersonal relationships that show compassion
- Ethics
- Means and ends—"more likely to appreciate for its own sake, an in an absolute way, the doing itself; they can often enjoy for its own sake the getting to some place as well as the arriving"[4]
- Humor
- Creativity
- Resistance to enculturation, "a certain inner detachment from the culture in which they are immersed"[5]

I found that a number of self-actualizing characteristics, including acceptance of self and others, an individual code of ethics, having a sense of duty/purpose (being problem-centered), perception of reality, spontaneity, creativity, and endeavoring to attain his/her full potential, were attributed by the teachers I interviewed as qualities that developed because of their meditation practice. These are all qualities that can help teachers have an edge in the classroom while helping them to avoid burnout. One of the teachers I analyzed taught in an inner-city middle school that was infamous for severe behavioral problems and low academic performance. Here is an excerpt from the personal narrative she wrote as part of the data for my study, describing her experience of how meditation had a positive impact on her as a middle-school teacher[6]:

Every morning, I would go to school with well laid out lesson plans and optimism, and every day my high hopes were dashed by so many distractions caused by young adults resistant to learning. I did okay, but not great. I knew that if I could stop feeling so much stress in the classroom, things would go much better. With my whole heart, I wanted to be there to make a difference for them.

This went on for about ten years. This whole time I was looking for better solutions…

I was listening to a radio talk show, and a meditation teacher was being interviewed about the benefits of silent mantra meditation. He talked about so many benefits that I couldn't remember all of them. But two things stuck in my mind. Meditation could release stress and unleash the potential of the meditator.

… Immediately, I made a phone call to schedule instruction in silent mantra meditation. My first meditations were amazing. I felt like a brand-new person.

The following Monday, I went to school and was wondering if this new found calmness would last. Surprisingly, the day went very well. I continued to meditate, and the week was the best week I ever remember in my teaching career.

I was so happy. This is what I dreamt about. Somehow, it became easy to come up with lessons and projects that captured my students' interest. And the most amazing quality I was able to manifest was the ability not to react, but to act. If a student tried to distract me or the class, somehow I would see it coming, and I was usually able to nip it in the bud spontaneously. I was becoming so flexible and aware that I surprised myself.

This went on for a few weeks. Then I thought, "I have this knack now, and I don't need to meditate anymore. I know that meditation teacher said to meditate twice a day for the rest of my life, but that's not for me. I don't need it anymore."

Guess what happened? When I stopped meditating, things were not good. I got irritable and stressed out and the kids seemed to be able to distract me. Things were just as they were before (meditating).

The bottom line here is that my teaching career forced me to meditate two times a day—once in the morning and once at noon—if I wanted to be a creative, inspiring teacher who acted calmly and very seldom reacted.

Another teacher I interviewed taught elementary school. Here's an excerpt from her narrative[7]:

I was born into a teaching family...My mom taught me much about teaching, both the good and the bad. She was a marvelous teacher who cared deeply about her students and their young adolescent challenges, but she was also plagued with alcoholism. She taught me how to care about my students. She also taught me that teaching was horribly stressful—even life threatening. She could not balance her life....

My father used to say over and over again, "Don't ever become a teacher. It'll make you crazy!!!"

...Professionally, I have found meditation to be extremely helpful. It has allowed me to balance my life much more effectively than my mother ever did. When a kid's behavior threatens to "make me crazy," I know it's time to fall back, meditate and let go; to remember that I don't have to get so emotionally agitated. I'm able to maintain my cool and still regard a child with respect and kindness, but also with firmness. I am able to see the cup half full instead of the cup half empty. Most importantly, I am able to inspire people every day. I teach my students to value caring, kindness and thoughtfulness as well as academic achievement.

These narrative descriptions provide a glimpse into how these teachers perceived meditation having an impact upon their teaching and their interactions with students. Meditation fostered certain self-actualizing qualities, including creativity and being more problem-centered rather than ego-centered. Rob Nairn, a scholar of both psychology and Tibetan Buddhism, explains that we learn to meditate because "as human beings we have a greater potential than just living, eating, working, sleeping" and that there "is a deeper aspect of meditation, namely the self-actualization of our inner potential."[8] Meditation creates the conditions for self-actualization to occur. Meditation can help us to tap into our full potential and be the best versions of ourselves—professionally and personally.

What Other Research Has Discovered about Meditation and Teachers

The use of meditation and mindfulness-based interventions in schools has increased considerably, and more and more research is emerging to determine how exactly it can affect teachers and students. Research confirms that meditation not only positively affects teachers, it can reverberate out into the entire classroom. In fact, "Mindfulness is capable of increasing teacher job-satisfaction, and in turn, improving student outcomes."[9] One of the most popular issues being looked at is how mindfulness can affect stress and burnout in classroom teachers. According to the Cleveland Clinic, stress is the natural physical/psychological response to challenges and can become problematic when stressful events occur over a period of time without intervals of relief.[10] Stress creates a feeling of being overwhelmed, exhausted, or unable to cope with circumstances. Left unchecked, stress can lead to burnout. Burnout manifests as a lack of energy, excitement, or motivation in one's work and is described as a "prolonged response to chronic emotional and interpersonal stressors on the job, and is defined by the three dimensions of exhaustion, cynicism, and inefficacy."[11]

In addition to helping teachers cope with stress and burnout (as evidenced by a number of studies), practicing meditation and mindfulness is beneficial for teachers' overall well-being, including concepts such as self-compassion. The practice of meditation and mindfulness also increases teachers' present-moment awareness. Findings indicate that mindfulness can help teachers to pause and assess a situation before reacting to it.[12] For example, a group of teachers in one study described mindfulness as enabling them to be less reactive and to experience "slowing, stopping, and pausing" in order to "respond rather than to react."[13] Similarly, Mindfulness-Based Stress Reduction has been shown to be beneficial for reducing stress in teachers, including teachers who work with students with emotional and behavioral disorders.[14] Other research has demonstrated that mindfulness can improve teacher disposition, or what they call "habits of mind," by fostering a flexibility of attention (ability to shift back and forth between individual students and the class as a whole), emotion regulation, present-moment awareness, and non-judgment.[15]

Another important teacher disposition developed through meditation is the quality of forgiveness after a conflict with a student.[16] As a teacher, I think that the ability of being able to forgive a student is crucial for a number of reasons, including healing the relationship with the student, creating greater harmony in the classroom, and rising above the problem in order to focus on positive solutions. Ultimately, being able to forgive allows the teacher to let go and release the stress that is associated with a given student or situation. Forgiveness, though benefitting all involved, really helps the person who does the forgiving. In this way, teachers can release the negative residue of a problem and prevent it from lodging itself in the mind and body.

In 2020, a study investigating the impact of mindfulness meditation on female teachers in Italy during the Covid-19 outbreak and lockdown examined the effects of an 8-week Mindfulness-Oriented Meditation (MOM) course.[17] The study analyzed a sample group of 66 female teachers who took a baseline test to measure personality profiles and subsequently were separated into two groups—high resilience and low resilience—prior to beginning the 8-week MOM course. The first two sessions were conducted in person immediately prior to the lockdown in Italy. The remainder of the six sessions were conducted online with individual instructor support provided via email and phone calls. Pre-post-test findings suggest that the mindfulness intervention enabled both groups to show significant improvements in anxiety, depression, affective empathy, emotional exhaustion, psychological well-being, interoceptive awareness, and mindfulness levels, and the low-resilience group showed even greater improvement in depression and psychological well-being.

Other researchers examined the effects of mindfulness on teachers in war-torn Western Negev, Israel.[18] Utilizing a qualitative methodology of semi-structured interviews of 15 female Israeli teachers who participated in a two-year mindfulness program, researchers found increases in coping skills, self-compassion, being less reactive, and sharing coping strategies with students. This study shows the potential of meditation to help teachers cope with stress and conflict under severe circumstances and provides evidence of the impact over a longer period of time. If meditation can be helpful for teachers working within a war zone, it can be useful for helping teachers cope with all types of conflict.

However, it must be noted that a limitation of many studies on mindfulness in schools is that there are more female than male participants. A possible question is whether or not female teachers are inherently more forgiving and more compassionate. Or are there simply more female teachers, or are the majority of teachers who are willing to participate in mindfulness programs/studies female? These are interesting questions to consider, and more research needs to be done to examine the effects of meditation on different groups of teachers.

Meditation and Student Teaching

Meditation can even help student teachers cope with stress and increase their capacity for empathy toward their students. I've known a number of student teachers who entered their student teaching experiences feeling excited and passionate about what they were going to teach and how they were going to connect with their students only to quickly feel defeated and overwhelmed with the workload, stress, and behavioral problems they encountered in the classroom. Some student teachers end up leaving before the end of the semester or crawl to the finish line and vow never to teach again. No matter how successful someone is in their college courses and how enthusiastic they are about becoming a teacher, the experience of student teaching is the real litmus test.

There is promising evidence, however, that meditation can help student teachers. In a study examining the effects of loving kindness meditation on student teachers, researchers gathered data from 70 participants who were student teaching in mainly elementary and middle school settings.[19] Participants were divided into two groups: the experimental group received instruction on loving kindness meditation and began meditating the first week, and the control group didn't begin instruction and practice of loving kindness meditation until week 6. (Group A meditated for 12 weeks, and Group B meditated for 6 weeks.) Both groups completed the Interpersonal Reactivity Index (IRI) and the Outcome Questionnaire 45.2 at different points, including baseline tests and post-tests. Both groups showed lower stress after 6 weeks of practice; however, the group that meditated for 12 weeks showed a continued decrease in stress from week 6 to 12. Levels of empathy in both groups of student teachers also increased after 6 weeks of meditating, but again the group of student teachers who meditated for 12 weeks continued to show increased levels of empathy. This study provides evidence in support of long-term meditation practice and indicates that the longer one meditates, the more effective it is for both reducing stress and increasing empathy. This is promising not just for student teachers but for teachers of all levels of experience.

Bottom Line

Yes, teachers already have too much to do. Yes, teachers have already endured many training programs and continuing education courses. *But*, if teachers do just one more training program, they should consider learning and practicing meditation. There is concrete research- based evidence demonstrating that meditation can improve the lives of teachers of all levels and years of experience (and benefit their students) by

- Reducing stress
- Decreasing burnout
- Increasing compassion, forgiveness, and empathy
- Increasing creativity and problem-solving skills
- Decreasing anxiety, depression, and emotional exhaustion
- Increasing present-moment awareness and positivity
- Increasing one's overall sense of well-being
- Contributing to qualities of self-actualization

Here's what's really compelling: Unlike most training programs for teachers, meditation is a practice that can have long-term, beneficial outcomes for teachers' personal lives, extending well beyond the classroom. A teacher might not be able to see the practical applications of learning to write better standardized test questions in their personal lives, but in practicing meditation, teachers will find countless possibilities for enriching their own lives. Meditation practice is an investment not just in the teacher but in the whole person. Teachers who meditate are investing in their future, and school districts who support their teachers in learning and practicing meditation are matching that contribution.

Notes

1 Maslow, A. H. (1987). *Motivation and personality* (3rd ed.). New York: Addison, Wesley, Longman.
2 Ibid. p. 138.
3 Ibid. p. 138.
4 Ibid. p. 141.
5 Ibid. p. 141.
6 Klein, L. (2008). *Developing higher consciousness: The effects of mantra meditation on the development of self-actualizing qualities in teachers*. Pittsburgh, PA: Duquesne University. pp. 130–132.
7 Ibid. pp. 114–116.
8 Nairn, R. (2001). *Diamond mind: A psychology of meditation*. Boulder: Shambhala. pp. 10–11.
9 Zarate, K., Maggin, D. M., & Passmore, A. (2019). Meta-analysis of mindfulness training on teacher well-being. *Psychology in the Schools*, 56(10), 1700–1715. p. 1711. https://doi.org/10.1002/pits.22308.

10 Cleveland Clinic. (1/28/2021, 2021-last update). Stress [Homepage of Cleveland Clinic], [Online]. Available: https://my.clevelandclinic.org/health/articles/11874-stress [March 2021].

11 Maslach, C., Schaufeli, W.B., & Leiter, M.P. (2001). Job burnout. *Annual Review of Psychology, 52*(1), 397–422.

12 Sharp, J. E., & Jennings, P.A. (2016). Strengthening teacher presence through mindfulness: What educators say about the cultivating awareness and resilience in education (CARE) program. *Mindfulness, 7*, 209–218.

13 Mackenzie, E. R., Fegley, S., Stutesman, M., & Mills, J. (2020). Present-moment awareness and the prosocial classroom: Educators' lived experience of mindfulness. *Mindfulness, 11*, 2755–2764. p. 2759.

14 Haydon, T., Alter, P., Hawkins, R., & Kendall Theado, C. (2019). "Check yourself": Mindfulness-based stress reduction for teachers of students with challenging behaviors. *Beyond Behavior, 28*(1), 55–60. https://doi.org/10.1177/1074295619831620.

15 Roeser, R. W., Skinner, E., Beers, J., & Jennings, P. A. (2012). Mindfulness training and teachers' professional development: An emerging area of research and practice. *Child Development Perspectives, 6*(2), 167–173. https://doi.org/10.1111/j.1750-8606.2012.00238.x.

16 Ibid.; Taylor, C., Harrison, J., Haimovitz, K., Oberle, E., Thomson, K., Schonert-Reichl, K., & Roeser, R. W. (2016). Examining ways that a mindfulness-based intervention reduces stress in public school teachers: A mixed-methods study. *Mindfulness, 7*, 115–129.

17 Matiz, A., Fabbro, F., Paschetto, A., Cantone, D., Paolone, A. R., & Crescentini, C. (2020). Positive impact of mindfulness meditation on mental health of female teachers during the COVID-19 outbreak in Italy. *International Journal of Environmental Research and Public Health, 17*(6450), 1–22.

18 Litvak-Hirsch, T., & Lazar, A. (2020). The contribution of long-term mindfulness training on personal and professional coping for teachers living in a conflict zone: A qualitative perspective. *International Journal of Environmental Research and Public Health, 17*(4096), 1–9.

19 Csaszar, I. E., Curry, J. R., & Lastrapes, R. E. (2018). Effects of loving kindness meditation on student teachers' reported levels of stress and empathy. *Teacher Education Quarterly, 45*(4), 93–116. https://www.jstor.org/stable/26762171.

5

Critiques and Caveats about Meditation and Mindfulness

Simple Yet Complex

Everyone's an expert.

> *All you have to do is focus on your breathing, right?*
> *Yeah, I have an app I listen to. I guess it helps.*
> *Oh, I do mindfulness with my students all the time. I play chill music for them, we lower the lights, they close their eyes, and we breathe.*
> *I just play YouTube videos for my classes, and they meditate with them.*

Just as adults think they can teach elementary classes simply because they were students themselves for years, many people think they can teach meditation or mindfulness simply because they sat through visualizations in a yoga class or once learned how to meditate. As any elementary teacher will tell you, there's a lot more involved with learning to teach than meets the eye, and teaching meditation is the same way.

During the Covid pandemic, the number of meditation and mindfulness instructors seemed to grow at alarming rates. People who never taught mindfulness before came out of the woodwork offering online workshops for people of all ages to learn mindfulness and meditation. I get it. There was clearly a need for stress management as we were in the great unknown of what our future was going to look like. Anxiety permeated every sphere of life. And let's face it: people needed money.

Social media posts advertising online courses in meditation and mindfulness popped up like weeds. To my knowledge, these good-natured folks didn't have any formal training or certifications in teaching mindfulness or meditation, but now they were teaching it. One online class I came across was teaching mindfulness to children with bottles of alcohol inadvertently in the background. I'm sure these folks meant well. I'm sure that they had taken yoga classes, read some books, listened to some apps about mindfulness, and truly believed that it would be easy enough to replicate. Again, people needed to fulfill the need to work at a time when our lives were turned upside down.

However, the concerns over having a qualified teacher for meditation or mindfulness started before the Covid pandemic, and they continue now. It seems like most people have heard of mindfulness, and many have experimented with it. But have they had the best results? Have they had proper instruction? There are countless apps and books about meditation and mindfulness, but ideally, it should be taught "face-to-face" by a trained mindfulness teacher.[1] According to Harvard neuroscientist Sara Lazar, "The most important thing, if you're going to try it, is to find a good teacher. Because it's simple, but it's also complex. You have to understand what's going on in your mind. A good teacher is priceless."[2] I believe that if meditation is to have the greatest benefits for you, the teacher you select should be highly trained to teach meditation.

Critiques and Caveats of Meditation

It's important to note that although there is a growing body of research supporting meditation for the mainstream, there are also critiques that challenge the Westernized form of meditation practices. Some argue that mindfulness has been commodified and used for questionable reasons in secular settings.[3] There has been criticism of mindfulness being potentially unethically used by the military and corporations for their own gains.[4] (I can't help but think of the movie *The Men Who Stare at Goats* based on the book by the same title by Jon Ronson when considering how the military could use mindfulness techniques to create super soldiers.[5]) Others argue that secularized forms of meditation promoting the idea of being in the present moment are flawed and misleading as the present moment is a moving target and fails to adequately address different levels of suffering.[6]

Some call for more scrutiny of research that makes claims about the benefits of mindfulness and meditation to avoid harming and misleading the public.[7] Arguments concerning the potential adverse effects of meditation, including triggering past trauma, have also been presented. However, these adverse effects are similar to the negative effects of other psychological treatments. Participants who reported experiencing meditation-related adverse effects also expressed that they were pleased to have practiced meditation and that ultimately these adverse effects are not typically long-term.[8] The key is transparency and ensuring that people are made aware of possible adverse effects of meditation prior to starting a program.[9] If someone is under the care of a therapist or psychologist/psychiatrist, they should discuss learning meditation with their health-care professional and receive approval from their health-care provider before starting any program in meditation. For example, certain mindfulness practices involve tapping into our inner feelings, sensations, and emotions. Not everyone may be prepared to do this. If someone has experienced trauma, they may need additional support or adapted practices.

Meditation teachers must be properly trained and prepared for helping students to cope with possible adverse effects.[10] With the ubiquity of mindfulness and meditation, many people seem to be self-professed practitioners and/or teachers because they use an app or read a visualization script they found online. They have no formal training in meditation. Proper teacher training is imperative in addressing the concerns of meditation programs and certain competencies need to be met by teachers of meditation and mindfulness.[11] For example, in the United Kingdom, the British Association of Mindfulness-Based Approaches (BAMBA) has a listing of registered mindfulness teachers who have fulfilled certain requirements, including course work, supervision with observations, and teaching practice.

Some critics offer a cautionary word about the incorporation of meditation and mindfulness programs for different populations such as teachers. These critics believe that the use of these types of practice might not be as effective or ethical as the media and even legitimate research studies purport. For example, some question the motivation behind introducing mindfulness to a school or work setting as contributing to the commodification of mindfulness, or as Terry Hyland calls it "McMindfulness."[12] Some critics question if teachers are being encouraged to practice mindfulness as a way to learn how to just be quiet and deal with the current status of education rather than address the actual problems.[13] Others acknowledge that mindfulness programs for teachers might be perceived as part of "a neoliberal agenda of 'resilience' in the face of socio-political adversity."[14] Other key criticisms of Western secular mindfulness programs include the questions of cultural appropriation, the failure to recognize its religious/spiritual roots, and the over-promising of programs that "often guarantee nearly instant results and provide little or no cultural or spiritual context."[15]

Even though I've delineated these critiques about meditation and mindfulness, I am a staunch advocate of meditation and mindfulness practices. I fully believe that meditation can be beneficial for most people. I am simply presenting a counterargument here. Even though there is an abundance of benefits for the body and mind, there are some things to take into consideration before jumping into any mindfulness or meditation program. These things include finding a trained meditation teacher, getting approval from your health-care provider if you are under psychiatric care, and being realistic with your expectations.

Sorry, There's No Rubric for Assessing Your Meditation Experience

As educators, we have been trained to develop exact criteria for judging whether or not someone has appropriately accomplished an assignment or a project. We have become really adept at creating checklists with point values attached that determine if all facets of the learning objectives have been met and demonstrated clearly. A score above a certain percentage will pass; a score below a certain percentage equals failure. Meditation does not play by these rules.

It's important to understand that not everyone will experience the same things when meditating. That's okay. There's no one "right" way to experience meditation. There is no set checklist of what you *should* have experienced and how you *should* feel during your meditation. This is especially true during the early phase of learning how to meditate. After I first learned to meditate, I had this feeling of peace, an absence of fear that I never remembered having before. My husband recalls that during his first meditation session, his eyes watered profusely. He felt a great release of stress from his body that was released through his tears. Some people will have an instant, profound experience of releasing stress and tension upon their first meditation session, whereas others might not feel much of anything during their first meditations. Still others might feel more agitated after their first sessions because they are allowing their minds and bodies to relax in a way that they aren't used to.

If you don't have an immediate and profound response to meditating when you learn, that's okay. Again, this is why working with an actual meditation teacher is so crucial. If you are working with a trained teacher, you can have conversations about what you're feeling. Without a meditation teacher to work with, someone might try meditation, not have the experience they thought they should have, and simply give up on trying to meditate. They could be walking away from a practice that could actually be quite beneficial for them. A trained teacher can help you to navigate the process of learning, offer support, and provide adaptations as needed.

Approaching meditation with the mindset that everyone will have a different experience—especially early on in meditating—is essential for accepting yourself and for getting the most out of the practice. The last thing you want is to feel like a failure at meditating. Stressing out about not attaining the exact results you *thought* you should have right away defeats the entire point of meditation. If you go into learning how to meditate with the mindset that you should experience an exact outcome, then you could very well be disappointed. As my meditation teacher told me, even if you don't feel that you are going "deep" during a meditation, you are still releasing stress from your body. The key is to stick with it. Some people might get frustrated because thoughts or emotions keep popping into their head while they're meditating. This is perfectly natural. They think that because they weren't able to make their mind quiet, they have failed somehow. The goal is not to eradicate thoughts or to make your mind go blank. It's more about having an awareness of the thoughts, just allowing them to be, and gently returning the attention to the meditation support.

In a world of instant gratification, the effects of meditation do not always promptly appear on our doorstep like our one-click food or shoe order. Meditation adheres to the ancient laws of being and does not conform to our conditioned impatience. The more you practice meditation and the more consistent you are with your practice, the more you will begin to notice a shift in yourself. The shift is often subtle. Sometimes *you* don't even recognize the shift at first, but those around you will begin to notice it. Over time, you will start to observe that you are *noticing* more. You will start to become more aware of your surroundings, of nature, of how you are *feeling* in each moment, and *why* you are having certain feelings. In a very natural way, you may begin to develop a greater sense of the feelings of others, which can lead to increased compassion and understanding. You also develop a greater mindset of compassion for yourself. A certain level of objectivity arises that enables you to begin to be less reactive and wiser in your responses to stress and conflict. You find yourself having an increased sense of stillness. These qualities will emerge over time. The results of meditation are cumulative. Be patient with yourself and trust the process.

Notes

1 Choden and Regan-Addis, H. (2018). *Mindfulness based living course*. Winchester: O Books. p. 6.
2 Schulte, B. (2015, May 26). Harvard neuroscientist: meditation not only reduces stress, here's how it changes your brain. *The Washington Post*. Inspired Life. https://www.washingtonpost.com/news/inspired-life/wp/2015/05/26/harvard-neuroscientist-meditation-not-only-reduces-stress-it-literally-changes-your-brain/ (Accessed on October 27, 2019). ISSN https://www.washingtonpost.com/news/inspired-life/wp/2015/05/26/harvard-neuroscientist-meditation-not-only-reduces-stress-it-literally-changes-your-brain/
3 Hyland, T. (2015). McMindfulness in the workplace: Vocational learning and the commodification of the present moment. *Journal of Vocational Education & Training*, *67*(2), 219–234. https://doi.org/10.1080/13636820.2015.1022871
4 Barrett, T., Harris, V., & Nixon, G. (Ed.). (2019). *Mindful heroes: Stories of journeys that changed lives*. Aberdeen, Scotland: Inspired By Learning.
5 Heslov, G. (Director). (2009). *The men who stare at goats* (Film). Smokehouse Pictures.
6 Purser, R. (2015). The myth of the present moment. *Mindfulness*, *6*, 680–686.
7 Van Dam, N. T., van Vugt, M. K., Vago, D. R., Schmalzl, L., Saron, C. D., Olendzki, A., ... Meyer, D. E. (2018). Mind the hype: A critical evaluation and prescriptive agenda for research on mindfulness and meditation. *Perspectives on Psychological Science*, *13*(1), 36–61. https://doi.org/10.1177/1745691617709589.
8 Aizik-Reebs, A., Shoham, A., & Bernstein, A. (2021). First, do no harm: An intensive experience sampling study of adverse effects to mindfulness training. *Behaviour Research and Therapy*, *145*, 103941. https://doi.org/10.1016/j.brat.2021.103941; Britton, W. B., Lindahl, J. R., Cooper, D. J., Canby, N. K., & Palitsky, R. (2021). Defining and measuring meditation-related adverse effects in mindfulness-based programs. *Clinical Psychological Science*, *9*(6), 1185–1204. https://doi.org/10.1177/2167702621996340; Schlosser, M., Sparby, T., Vörös, S., Jones, R., & Marchant, N. L. (2019). Unpleasant meditation-related experiences in regular meditators: Prevalence, predictors, and conceptual considerations. *PloS One*, *14*(5), e0216643. http://dx.doi.org/10.1371/journal.pone.0216543.

9 Goldberg, S. B., Lam, S. U., Britton, W. B., & Davidson, R. J. (2021). Prevalence of meditation-related adverse effects in a population-based sample in the United States, *Psychotherapy Research*, *32*(3), 291–305. https://doi.org/10.1080/10503307.2021.1933646.

10 Treleaven, D. A. (2018). *Trauma-sensitive mindfulness: Practices for safe and transformative healing*. New York: Norton.

11 Crane, R.S., Kuyken, W., Williams, J.M.G., Hastings, R.P., Cooper, L., & Fennell, M.J.V. (2012). Competence in teaching mindfulness-based courses: Concepts, development and assessment. *Mindfulness*, *3*, 76–84.

12 Hyland, McMindfulness in the workplace.

13 McCaw, C. T. (2020). Mindfulness 'thick' and 'thin'— a critical review of the uses of mindfulness in education. *Oxford Review of Education*, *46*(2), 257–278. https://doi.org/10.1080/03054985.2019.1667759.

14 Wigelsworth, M., & Quinn, A. (2020). Mindfulness in schools: An exploration of teachers' perceptions of mindfulness-based interventions. *Pastoral Care in Education*, *38*(4), 293–310. p. 307. https://doi.org/10.1080/02643944.2020.1725908.

15 Surmitis, K. A., Fox, J., & Gutierrez, D. (2018). Meditation and appropriation: Best practices for counselors who utilize meditation. *Counseling and Values*, *63*(1), 4–16. p. 8. https://doi.org/10.1002/cvj.12069.

Part II

Stories from My Career and How Meditation Played a Vital Role

Part II

6

The Transformation of an Introvert

How Meditation Calmed My Anxiety and Helped Me to Blossom

Elementary Introvert

For most of my life, I never felt like I quite fit in. As a kid, I was extremely introverted to the point where my third-grade teacher recommended me for counseling because I didn't socialize. It didn't help that I was terrified of her! She used to paddle students in front of the class for all sorts of infractions. She paraded that wooden paddle around like a trophy. I'll call her Miss Frog because she collected all things frog. She *obsessed* over frogs. Miss Frog dressed in golf clothes and penny loafers. She had a huge wart on her face, which, according to elementary legend, she got from kissing a frog. She gave hideous amounts of grammar homework. There was no frivolity in her classroom.

Miss Frog's assessment of me being an introvert was correct, but even in her attempt to help me, she caused me more anxiety. She had the school social worker—a tall, gray-haired older man dressed in a suit—come to the classroom door and loudly announce to the class that he needed to see Lisa Klein. All eyes shifted to me. I was in hell. Who was this old man wearing a suit who wanted to see me? I had no idea what this was about. Nobody gave me any warning that somebody was going to be talking with me in school or why. Reluctantly, I got up and walked into the hallway feeling my entire class stare at me. For someone who is an introvert, this was the worst way to introduce counseling. The social worker took me down the hall to an old, small storage room that had a conference table wedged in the middle of it and packed shelves around the perimeter of the room. It was a dingy and makeshift conference room. He closed the door, and I felt great panic as he asked me to have a seat.

He proceeded to tell me that I could tell him anything I was feeling. I could be completely honest with him. How did I feel about my teacher? He promised he wouldn't tell her what I said. How did I feel about school, about home, about my friends? Did I have many friends? Lots of questions. I just remember sitting there being very nervous and unsure of why I was there and why this stranger was asking all of these questions. I just kept saying that everything was fine. Even if something was wrong, I wasn't about to tell this stranger. I was only a kid, but I had some common sense. This was before the "Stranger Danger" movement, but there was no way that I was disclosing anything to this stranger who in my mind had no need to know.

I went home from school that day and tore into my mom about the entire experience. Honestly, I don't even think the school told her they were having the social worker talk with me. I was crying because I was so upset to be singled out in front of my class and to have to be alone with this strange man and to have felt that something was wrong with me. My mom, who has always been my defender, called the school and immediately put an end to the tall, gray-haired man pulling me out of class.

This was a different era in education. The teacher down the hall whom I had two years later (whom I actually really liked) used to throw kids across desks and slam kids into lockers. The sound of a kid being thrashed into lockers could be heard down the entire hallway. At least he did this to boys only, so I felt safer when I had him. Times clearly, and thankfully, have changed. I was already an introvert, and these teaching practices didn't help.

Faking It until I Made It in Middle School and High School

My entire childhood I suffered from horrible anxiety. I remember being in middle school and high school and needing to take Pepto Bismol many mornings because I was sick to my stomach with nerves. In high school, I figured out how to hide my anxiety better. My mom gave me a helpful piece of advice for every time I was nervous to try something new. She told me to just do my best and "fake it 'til you make it." This helped me to force myself to be more outgoing. I joined different clubs and activities, including the marching band, which was a game changer for me socially—Yes! I was a band geek and proud of it! I had a family of friends in the band and that led me to participating in other activities and making more friends. By my senior year, I was Vice President of the Senior Class and Homecoming Queen. I was a million miles away from that introverted third grader who was truly terrified of my teachers and the other students.

But guess what? I was still suffering from anxiety, except nobody knew it. I'm not sure I even understood it really. The undercurrent of tension and anxiety that bubbled in me had just been part of my life for so many years that I don't know if I even fully recognized it as anything other than something that was just part of who I was. It had just become part of my framework. I had brown hair, I had hazel eyes, and I had a constant undercurrent of nervous vibration that ran through me. Perfectly normal. I had experienced this undercurrent of anxiety for so long that I didn't know that life could exist without it. I became really good at living with it and functioning quite successfully in many ways. Looking back now, I realize that it was quite dysfunctional because even though I appeared to have it all and to be well on my way to having a successful life, I was really living in fear. I feared almost everything from failure to being ridiculed. This perpetual tinge of anxiety was my constant companion.

Centering Myself in College

When I started college, I took a couple of courses that began to spark an interest in meditation in me. I remember my freshman philosophy class discussing Eastern belief systems and learning about meditation, the Buddha, and reading Hermann Hesse's *Siddhartha*. Hmmm. I had never heard of these beliefs before, but now concepts such as the "Middle Way" made a lot of sense to me. Then I took a class on Human Morality taught by a former nun. She was one of the most liberal and provocative professors I ever had. She engaged us in conversations pertaining to morality, sex, religion, one's personal connection with God, and what it meant to be spiritual. On my own, I started to read books about psychology and philosophy and realized that there was something out there I needed to find. I didn't quite know what exactly at that point, but I sensed something starting to stir in me. I was dating a guy who attended a neighboring university. I was telling him about these classes and about the books I was reading. He looked at me and said, "You need to meet my mom." I blushed. He wanted me to meet his mom? He quickly followed it with "She meditates. You should learn how to meditate."

The following school year, I learned to meditate. I discuss the experience in my TEDx Talk of when I first learned to meditate.[1] I walked out of the building at the retreat where I had been meditating, started to walk across the parking lot, and stopped in my tracks. I was having a strange experience and wanted to see what I was feeling. What was going on in me? This felt very weird. Good but strange. Then I realized that it wasn't *what* I was feeling but rather *what I wasn't* feeling. Something was missing. For the first time in my memory, I didn't feel anxious. That feeling of dread, of worry, of fear was replaced by a feeling of emptiness. I know that might sound bizarre and not really a good thing, but actually that sensation of emptiness allowed for an openness, a feeling of expansion. There was a feeling of calm, of relief, of happiness. It was the kind of happiness that is there for no reason. The tinge of anxiety was replaced by the calm stillness of happiness. So this was how life could feel? This is what not being anxious feels like? I never wanted to let that feeling go.

Throughout the rest of college, I continued to meditate. I found that I could meditate almost anywhere. I meditated in the school library or on a bench outside on nice days. Ideally, I meditated back at home in my quiet room, but I was pretty good at squeezing in a meditation wherever I was. It just looked like I was sitting up with my eyes closed, like I just dozed off. When I started teaching, it became a bit more difficult to meditate twice a day because of my schedule and being totally inundated with work, but I did my best to meditate when I could. I still attended regular weekend meditation retreats, but I did slip up in my daily meditations those first few years. Meditation is so easy to do, but it's also extremely difficult because it requires discipline and dedication. The difference in how I felt on the days that I meditated compared with the days I didn't meditate convinced me that I needed to make meditating a priority.

Oh, and the guy I was dating who suggested I learn meditation, I married after college, and we have been married ever since. We have also been meditating together ever since.

The Power of Stories

I took some graduate classes in Rome, Italy years ago. In one of the classes, we discussed leadership and how to best convey ideas. The professor explained that the use of the narrative was a powerful way to communicate larger concepts to any audience. He noted a number of historical leaders and teachers who used storytelling to share information, insights, and lessons. This resonated with me right away as I thought about how I learned best and the type of teachers I enjoyed the most. Rather than just providing didactic instruction on a given topic, the teachers who imparted some sort of personal connection or illustrative story always awakened a passion for learning in me. I think that's why I enjoyed teaching literature so much. I loved being able to share stories that taught different lessons or made the students think about the thematic relevance of the story in relation to their own lives. Both fiction and non-fiction stories have the power to achieve this.

I wanted my students to be intentional about what they read, and I wanted them to determine on their own why we read stories. Their first assignment of the school year was to come up with an original quote answering the question:

What Is the Purpose of Literature?

They were instructed to type up or creatively write out their quote and sign their name to it. I wanted them to own their thoughts. We hung the quotes up in the room and used their original quotes as a springboard for our conversations about both fiction and non-fiction selections that we read throughout the year. After they hung up their quotes, I shared my quote:

> *Literature provides us with the eyes to peer into the soul of every time period.*
>
> ~L. Klein

The following vignettes I will be sharing with you are non-fiction. These are actual experiences that I've had as a teacher. My intention in sharing these narratives of my teaching career is to provide the reader with the eyes to peer into the lived experience of a teacher who taught in an American public high school from 1997 to 2020 and who credits the practice of meditation with helping her survive and thrive as a teacher. The high school where I taught was an eclectic mix of middle-class and low-income families. It had a large population of English language learners and two housing projects that fed into the district. I could just simply tell you how meditation affected me as a teacher, but I think it's better that these stories show you how meditation helped me to be healthier and happier even during times of difficulty.

A Word about the Stories

I will share representative vignettes from the beginning, middle, and final years of my 23-year teaching career. I will provide a reflection of the vignettes that will highlight the connection between my meditation practice and my professional experience. Because of the potential arguments that my teaching experience could have been a factor in my ability to handle stress and conflict in the classroom or that my diet could have contributed to my health and well-being, I aim not to draw a direct cause/effect relationship but rather to provide a glimpse into my life as a teacher who also practiced meditation for the duration of my career, offering my insights into how meditation has affected me.

Please note that all names have been changed for ethical reasons.

How the Vignettes Connect to the Research

The vignettes in this section support some of the main findings discovered within the research that was presented in Part I. These key areas are listed in the order in which they were first noticed during my teaching career. Creativity was one of the first areas to be affected by my meditation practice. Also, early on in my teaching career, I noticed how meditation influenced my ability to handle stress and conflict within the classroom. During the middle of my career, I increasingly observed how meditation affected my physical and mental health. At this time, I also began experiencing synchronicity and an increase in qualities of self-actualization. In the later years of my career, all of these areas continued to emerge, and I also began to perceive more of the long-term effects of meditation, including a slowing of the aging process and higher levels of awareness. In summation, the following key areas will be demonstrated within the vignettes:

- ◆ Creativity
- ◆ Ability to handle stress/conflict in the classroom
- ◆ Physical and mental health and well-being
- ◆ Synchronicity
- ◆ Qualities of self-actualization
- ◆ Long-term effects of meditation, including effects on aging and a higher level of awareness

A Brief Explanation of My Meditation Technique

The meditation practice I will be referring to in the following vignettes is a silent mantra meditation technique rooted in an Indian tradition, dating back about 5,000 years. This technique is taught one-on-one with a trained meditation teacher who provides the student with a personalized Sanskrit mantra, which is repeated silently during the meditation. It is recommended that one meditate twice a day for 20 minutes each time. One can sit on a chair or cushion, but one's back should be straight, and the hands should rest comfortably on one's lap. This technique fosters a deep level of rest for both the mind and the body. I was 19 years old when I learned this technique, and I have been practicing it ever since—for 30 years. The following vignettes provide a glimpse into my journey as a teacher and how meditation played a part along the way.

Note

1 Klein, L. (2016). *TEDx talk, meditation: Teaching from within.* https://www.youtube.com/watch?v=o2JPumXZtlw

7

The Early Years of Teaching

A Rough Start

Okay, I give this career five years. I can do anything for five years, right? I've invested all this time and money to become a teacher, so I have to do this—for now. I need to shut up and know I'm lucky to have a job right out of school. Summers off. I give myself a pep talk as I load my three-tiered cart that I need to take with me to teach five classes, four different courses, in four different rooms throughout the day because I'm the new guy and there aren't enough classrooms. What am I teaching to 9 Core today? I blank. I have no idea. Last night, I had time to prep for only the other three courses I teach. Ugh. I need to go to the bathroom. Again. I have a nervous tummy. It's the worst manifestation of anxiety. Why can't my skin just get blotchy or something? *No*, I have to experience the runs every time I get anxious. And that's every morning I'm here. I'm sure the other teachers have noticed how much time I spend in the bathroom every morning. I'm rail thin from being so sick to my stomach at the start of each day.

I'm living in the amygdala. Only fight or flight going on here. And guilt. I've been meditating for a couple of years, but it isn't easy anymore. When I was a student, meditating in the library between classes was easy. I can't meditate now. No time. I just have to power through this agony and impossible workload.

I don't even have time in between classes to decompress and go to the bathroom because I'm always gauntlet-style running through the crowded, narrow halls to my next room. Students bumping into me, knocking stuff off the cart constantly. So, by the time I arrive at my next class, chaos has usually already staked claim to the room. "Ms. Klein, Mike's running around on the roof" is my greeting as I frantically rush into the room pushing my cart.

"Shit." I mutter to myself as I run to the window and yell out for the student to get back in from the roof. This kid—well, he's more like 17, so he's old enough to know better—does this all the time. Then, as I'm yelling for him to get off the roof, he runs the perimeter faster, laughing at me each time. He's such a pain in my ass, but if he falls off, I'm responsible. Even if he doesn't fall off, somebody driving by is going to see him and report it. Either way, there goes my evaluation. I continue to yell as he taunts me, running around. Another boy decides to be "helpful" and join him on the roof. There are no phones in the room for me to call the office, and I was already warned by many teachers and administrators that reporting things to the office will only make me look like I have no control of my classes. And I don't.

Did I mention this was my best class? My only academic class all day. Realizing the inequalities of teaching was a baptism by fire. The building principal (I'll call him Mr. Bronson) hated me before he even met me. I was coming up from the middle school where I was a permanent substitute after finishing my student teaching in the fall. The middle school principal loved me but unfortunately didn't have any openings. When she found out the high school had an opening, she used all her power to see to it I got an interview and the endorsement from Central Administration. (Side note: the middle school principal and the high school principal hated each other. The middle school principal was held in much higher esteem in the eyes of Central Administration and the School Board, so *her* endorsement of me being hired for *his* building really infuriated him.) The end result: another English teacher and I were both hired at the same time. The high school principal gave the other teacher her own classroom, only two different courses to plan for and teach and only two grade levels, and all five of her classes were the academic and honors classes. I had to run in between four different classrooms, plan for and teach four different courses each day (five classes total), teach three different grade levels, and instruct mainly the low-performing, troubled students. Our teaching days looked nothing alike. We got paid the same, but I was doing three times the amount of work. At the end of the day, she left looking impeccably put together strolling to her car, while I looked disheveled, haggard, and hunched over dragging myself to mine.

Even though daily meditation was difficult because of time, I did still attend meditation retreats on the weekends several times throughout the year. These proved to be extremely beneficial for me as a new teacher. A weekend retreat did wonders for allowing my mind and body to recuperate after the stress of teaching. I could start a new school week in a much healthier place emotionally. One of the biggest things I noticed was meditation helping me to be more creative and to problem-solve certain issues I was encountering in my classes. For example, as a new teacher, I needed to be observed for three days in a row as part of my formal observation process. Knowing that Mr. Bronson already wasn't a fan of mine, I was determined that I had to impress him even more. But how? I was sooooooooo nervous of this impending observation because I was being critiqued on the lesson creation, write up, delivery, student behavior—everything! Every aspect of this lesson had to be structured and executed with academic rigor and pedagogical precision. I fretted over what to do for weeks.

Even though I didn't have time to go away for a meditation retreat, I knew I needed to. At the retreat, during one of the meditations, an idea for my formal observation lesson just popped into my head. Eureka! As part of the curriculum, I had to teach the Anglo-Saxon epic poem *Beowulf* to my senior students. During meditation, I had the idea of having students work in small groups to write original, modernized scripts of different sections of the poem and then perform those skits in front of the class. I could've picked any course I was teaching and any piece of literature for the observation, but this is what emerged as being the best idea.

I wrote up the lesson and submitted it. Students worked in groups and created scripts. The students were ready to perform their scripts, and Mr. Bronson sat stoically in the back, arms folded. The group with "Mike the roof-runner" in it started to beat the crap out of each other. Yes, they were "reenacting" a fight scene from the poem, but this was a bit too realistic. I tried to intervene, but my protests to their violent performance were overpowered by the cheers of the class. When a boy stood on the desk and threw a chair as part of the scene, I thought: "That's it. I'm fired."

I hesitantly looked over at my principal, and he was smiling ear to ear applauding. What?? Mr. Bronson actually liked this? At my follow-up meeting, he complimented me for creating a lesson so engaging that the whole class was captivated. He was extremely impressed and applauded my ability to take an ancient text and make it accessible for teenagers, "who would, no doubt, never forget learning about *Beowulf*."

From this moment, I learned to trust the ideas that came to me through meditation, and I continued to meditate—literally—on how to create and teach lessons and how to tackle dilemmas within the classroom. I made it a habit of thinking about a problem or a lesson before I began a meditation, and frequently an idea would come to me as I was meditating, or it would come to me shortly after I meditated. I started to keep little notebooks all around in the main places where I meditated. I still have a notebook in my nightstand for when I meditate in bed. I have notebooks in my office at home, where I also like to meditate. I used to keep notebooks in my school bag for when I meditated at school.

Epic Fail

A year or so later, I had another observation, and this one was a surprise observation. Most of my career, I had no idea what day or time a principal would show up to conduct my yearly, formal observation. Teachers would fret about this every time they saw a principal walk down the hallway. If you were extremely lucky, your formal observation would be conducted during the beginning of the year and then you felt a huge weight lifted from you the rest of the year. There were still the numerous times throughout the year when the principal would just pop into your room for 10–20 minutes and informally observe you. Administration called these "walk-throughs," but we called them "drive-bys" because however innocuous they were intended to be, they had the tendency to invoke panic. Inevitably, it often seemed to be the absolute worst day and class period for a principal to observe when he/she would nonchalantly saunter into the room with their notebook (later laptop) in hand and casually take a seat in the back of the room. Ugh.

In this particular instance of my "gotcha" observation, I had cafeteria duty the period before where a girl threw a large drink filled with ice across the cafeteria at another student. I intervened and told the girl she needed to clean up the drink. Screaming, she called me a "f---ing c--t" for the entire cafeteria to hear. Then the bell rang for the period to end. As students raced out of the cafeteria, I obviously needed to deal with this student. First, I had to calm the poor, older cafeteria lady who now had this huge mess to clean up before the next group of students arrived, and then I had to take this student to the social worker's office because they were working with her on a behavioral plan.

I was trying to do all of this as fast as I could because I had to get back up to the second floor and teach in 5 minutes. (It is truly miraculous how much a teacher can accomplish in 5 minutes. In my normal life, I can barely put on my shoes and coat in 5 minutes. When I taught, I was able to answer three student questions, go to the bathroom, run down the hall to grab papers from the faculty room, call up a presentation on my computer, and be back at my door to greet students for the next class, all in 5 minutes.) I was literally running as fast as I could to get to my next class period. I was at the bottom of the stairwell when the late bell rang. Crap. I was late. This was my worst class of the day, too. They would undoubtedly be beating the hell out of each other without me in the room. Just a few weeks before, I had to break up a fight between two students who got into a vicious physical altercation that started in the room and then tumbled out into the hallway, where luckily another teacher was able to help me. I raced as fast as I could up the stairs, ran full speed down the hall to my classroom, and arrived at my door barely able to breathe, expecting total chaos. Gasping for breath, I ran into the room and found the strangest site. Every one of my students was sitting up straight and quietly facing the front of the room. Eerie. What was going on? Then I looked back and saw the principal sitting with his arms crossed in the back of the room glaring at me. Dammit.

 I wanted to yell back to Mr. Bronson and tell him what just happened and why I was late, but he pointed to his watch and signaled that I needed to ignore him and start the lesson. Flustered, I realized that I had scheduled a workday for this class today because attendance was so sporadic and so many students were behind on everything and needed my help on an individual basis to get caught up because the marking period was ending. "Workdays," though realistically needed, were frowned upon, and certainly I didn't want my yearly formal observation to be based on a workday. All administration ever wanted to see was cooperative learning. Now, I very much appreciate and value cooperative learning and group projects, but there is a time and place for them. This class wasn't it. Physical altercations or screaming matches broke out every time I moved students into groups. I tried all sorts of configurations and strategies and different types of learning activities. The class was filled with volatile students, such as one kid who had recently brought up a test to me saturated in his blood and handed it to me saying, "Here's your fucking test." He had some sort of sharp object on him and, within minutes of having the test, cut his hand open until it bled enough to literally saturate the entire test in blood. (I didn't remember reading about this scenario in any of my teacher training textbooks.) Whole class and individualized instruction just worked better with this particular class, and the students indicated repeatedly this is what they preferred. I wasn't about to argue with them.

 I took a few breaths. I did my best to quickly center myself and then like lightening ran a few possible lesson ideas through my head. Bingo. There was a short non-fiction selection in their books about a plane crash in the Potomac River. We were scheduled to read it the following week, but I needed to shift gears quickly here. I hadn't actually read the selection yet (I know, I know), because I hadn't taught this course before, and with multiple courses to have to plan and prep for each day, sometimes I was just barely ahead of the students. Trying to remain calm and composed in this moment, I figured how hard could it be for me to quickly read through this short essay as the students were reading and create some higher-order thinking questions for a think-pair-share. Easy. No problem.

Unfortunately, the principal was very familiar with this older news story and delightedly got up and grabbed a book to read along. I struggled to read fast enough to also be able to move around the room and redirect students to stay on task. By the time we got to the think-pair-share questions, I was able only to skim the article. I managed to keep my cool and stay poised, but inside I felt like I was melting. The think-pair-share activity failed. In fact, it failed so badly that during my post-observation meeting, the principal called me out on how poor of a lesson it was. Because he was so familiar with the story, he felt like I needed to focus on other aspects of it. And why didn't the students work together better? Also, he told me that having an incident in the cafeteria was no excuse for being late for a class. Epic fail.

I'm not going to lie. That was a rough lesson. Everything about that day was horrible, and I wanted to cry. Maybe I did cry a little bit. Eventually, I waved my emotional surrender flag. I could've beat myself up for a long time about this day. I could've been quite self-destructive or have sunk into a deep pit of depression and anxiety. These emotions certainly were bubbling in me when I left school that day. I did feel like a failure and was anxious about my yearly evaluation. I went home, dropped down in my comfy spot, and meditated. Sometimes meditation helps you to get ready for a class. Sometimes meditation helps you to conduct a great lesson. And sometimes meditation helps you to heal from a day from hell. On this day, meditation helped me to lick my wounds, let go of a day that was disastrous, give myself some self-compassion, and move forward.

How Meditation Helped

Meditation doesn't eliminate the troubles in life. Difficulties beyond our control will still happen. Unpredictable student behavior or poorly timed principal visits could occur at any time. The workload that teachers have each day can make it impossible to be perfect every day, every class period. Occasionally, lessons fail. At times, we aren't prepared as much as we want to be. There are only so many hours in the day, and teachers have to juggle many different roles. Then there are times when we have everything perfectly planned out ready to go and unexpected challenges arise that throw everything out of whack.

Meditating at the end of a horrible day of teaching doesn't erase all of the events of that day, but it always helped me to process them better. Meditating helped me to release the stress from my body and lessened the burden of being held hostage to ruminating over bad days. Just to be clear, this didn't always happen overnight. Sometimes—especially in the early years of teaching—it took several days or weeks of meditating to release obsessing over more severe problems. Ultimately, however, meditation helped me to be kinder to myself and to let go of the emotions from that day, so that I could start again the next day with a more positive mindset than I would have otherwise.

8

From Fear to Love

More Stories from the Early Years

The Grandmother Approach

About a month into the school year, I'm called to a meeting with an emotional support teacher, the social worker, a guidance counselor, the principal, and a mother.

> Now Dillon is volatile. He has violent tendencies and a history of aggressive behavior. You are never to allow him to leave your room for any reason. Even if he says he needs to use the restroom. You'll have to find a security guard to escort him…. You also cannot stop him from leaving your room. He may become agitated and violent if you try to prevent him from leaving your room.

Okaaaaaay. I'm confused. Never allow him to leave my room but also don't try to stop him from leaving? Is this *The Twilight Zone*? Dillon is a senior this year. They've decided to try to place him in a regular education English classroom for the first time ever. He's been in an emotional support classroom every year previously. They believe I will be a good fit for Dillon; I'm young, cute, and friendly. I feel as if I'm the pretty damsel about to be sacrificed.

After teaching for a couple of years at this point, I knew how difficult it was to establish classroom expectations and a positive environment starting on day one only to then have a new student added to the class who upsets the entire ecosystem, causing disruptions and forcing you to start over again with classroom management training.

I explain that this is already a very challenging class with quite a few students who are already volatile.

You'll be fine. We know you can handle this.

I'm leery. I immediately go into survival mode. I head back to my classroom, take out the seating chart, and begin to strategize. Is there someone I can seat him by whom he won't fight with and who isn't already a huge behavioral problem themselves? And most importantly, I need to sit him as far away from me as possible. Ah, the back corner—the very last seat in the row by the window. Yes, perfect. That way if he becomes violent, I will be able to get to the door before he can reach me. (I know. That's not very enlightened thinking. What kind of self-centered teacher am I? I was a survivalist.)

So Dillon arrived in my class. Late. Without a pass. Six feet, six inches tall. Towering over my 5-foot, 4-inch self. Immediately, he set to work making a scene and causing disruptions. Great. I show him his seat knowing full well that he is not able to sit for more than a few minutes at a time. He'll need to walk around. My room is extremely small, completely full of students, with just barely a tiny walkway between each row and between my desk and the rest of the room. *And* he can't leave the room. *And* he's huge. The next few weeks are beyond difficult. The class is chaos most of the time. I can safely say that very little academic learning was occurring. I tried my best classroom management strategies. I tried to think back to all the educational theories I learned. I was sinking. The bright spot? The rest of the students were terrified of Dillon. So, one day when I was desperately trying to get the class calmed down and get everyone settled, Dillon witnessing my struggle, stood up, and yelled, "Okay, everyone, right now, shut the FUCK up!" It worked. They all looked at him with terror because they knew he would gladly beat the hell out of them, and they instantly became silent. I realized then that although he was extremely volatile, a distraction, and a severe behavioral problem himself, at least he liked me enough to make sure the other students listened to me.

I was still attending weekend meditation retreats throughout the year. On these retreats, we would meditate, participate in yoga classes, and discuss books pertaining to spiritual and psychological development. I remember on one of these retreats we discussed the topic of surrendering and relinquishing our need to control. Taking a walk with my meditation teacher, I explained my dilemma to her. As a teacher, I was supposed to control my classes. How could I relinquish control without total mayhem breaking out? I really struggled with this contradiction. I can't remember my mentor's exact words, but I remember her discussing how much I will be able to learn and grow through these challenges and that these difficulties are really opportunities. She also discussed the importance of not judging these students—we are all here to learn and grow, and we are all at different points in our development, so compassion is needed. These students are going through their own challenges. She said that by meditating more regularly, I would develop my compassion and understanding. Yes, there were rules they needed to follow, and I had to have expectations for their behavior for the health and safety of the entire class, but perhaps I could approach things differently? Was there a way I could move out of the fear and anxiety I had for these students?

I was skeptical. Everything she said made sense, but was that realistic? I was teaching students, who were—and I realize this is not a clinical, nor a politically correct term—crazy. Dillon was just one such student out of many students I had over the years who were severely troubled.

But, okay, how do I not become overwhelmed and react through fear with these students? I continued to meditate, and I made an effort to meditate more regularly. I'm not trying to sugar-coat my experiences and pretend that magically after meditating, rainbows and gumdrops filled my classes with happiness and joy. No, my students still had all their problems. Sometimes I still got angry with them. However, slowly, a realization took hold of me. If I was afraid, these students must really be afraid!

They obviously weren't afraid of *me*. But they were most definitely acting out of fear. I started to pause more when a student would misbehave. Instead of instantly reacting, I paused, and in that pause, I was able to see their fear. Many times these were tough students who appeared to be confident. And the more regularly I meditated, the more I began to detect subtleties in their behavior. I began to see sadness in some, loneliness, anger—and fear. Fear was the umbrella emotion. It was always linked with their anger. When they were afraid, they would get angry and act out or just shut down. What were they afraid of? Failure. They had other fears as well, but most of their negative behavior they expressed in class was linked to their fear of failure and the fear of losing face. They were afraid of failing English, failing all their courses, and failing out of school. Conversely, they were afraid of graduating from school and then needing to figure out life outside of these halls. Some students would get even more defiant and angry before a holiday break. Some feared being home more than they feared school.

When I was in a calmer state after meditating, I was better able to recognize the pain and fear in my students. Gradually, something started to shift in me. I began to act like a grandma. I was young, but instead of acting through power and trying to assert myself as being the one in charge (which, through self-reflection, I realize was my own fear), I began taking on grandma-like qualities. I eventually started calling it my "grandmotherly approach" to teaching. I embodied the personality of a sweet grandma who just wanted the best for her grandkid. Instead of yelling at a student to stop being disruptive and start doing his work, I would calmly walk over to his desk, squat down next to it, and in a pleasant voice ask him if he needed anything. What could I do to help him? Now, this sounds super obvious, but keep in mind, this was not necessarily a case where the student was even remotely doing what he was supposed to be doing. A normal reaction would 100% be to simply tell the student to stop their behavior and pay attention/be on task. But, when I would take the grandmotherly approach instead, the student would almost always instantly soften. Frequently, they would say, sorry, they just didn't know what to do or how to do something. Or they would say, "No, I'm good." And maybe just to make me go away, they would start the assignment. Or sometimes they would say something like "I'm sorry. I'm just really hungry. I didn't have breakfast." No problem, grandma always kept snacks in the room. Other times they might say they had a really rough night at home and they weren't able to concentrate. I could then quietly offer to write them a pass to go talk with their counselor.

I wasn't always in the right frame of mind to handle every classroom situation calmly. I made plenty of mistakes as a teacher. But the more regularly I meditated, the more I noticed I was able to be less reactive and more present to the needs of my students. When I got too busy with life and didn't meditate for a few days, I noticed a difference in how I reacted to my students and how I felt. I felt more agitated, less understanding, less patient—everything just felt more stressful. When I meditated more, I noticed that I had more patience, understanding, and compassion for my students. I felt less stressed, and even though conflict occurred in the class, I was able to have a clearer perspective of the situation. I had a better ability to not take their behavior personally. I developed a realization that the only way to counteract their fear was with love. Meditation helped me to transition from fear-based reactions to more loving, compassionate responses. This didn't happen overnight, but over time, there was a definite shift from fear to love or at least to acceptance.

Getting back to Dillon, with the help of another teacher, I found a solution to Dillon's need to walk around by enlisting him as my helper to deliver papers/messages to a nearby teacher in the department whenever I detected that he was at his breaking point and needed to move around. I had to break protocol to do this, but it really helped with managing his need for space. I developed a good relationship with Dillon, and I think that he appreciated my kindness. Unfortunately, before the end of the year, he was suspended from school for physically attacking another teacher. Years later, I heard he was in prison and probably would be spending the majority of his life behind bars. This still saddens me.

One of My Greatest Teachers

Before I had Dillon, I had another student in the beginning of my teaching career who, had I not had the support of meditation, probably would have caused me to leave teaching. He was a very troubled student who was in my ninth-grade core English class. I'll call him Billy. Billy was in ninth grade but, according to his age, should have been in 10th or 11th grade. He tortured me. Daily. I had him seventh period. I discovered quickly in my career that seventh period is the worst period of the day. It feels like it should be the end of the day, but it's not. Students always seemed the worst behaved during this class period.

Prior to computerized attendance, we used to get attendance sheets sent to our rooms halfway through the day that listed all of the students who were absent in the morning. Every day, I would grab the attendance bulletin and frantically skim through it hoping to find Billy's name on it. Ah, the relief when I would see his name on the absent list. I just might be able to survive the class that day. Then the sounds of agony that would escape from my lips when I would see him later that day sashaying through my classroom door. I even uttered openly on more than one occasion, "What are you doing here!? You're on the absent list!" He would give me a sadistic smile with his broken-toothed mouth and sarcastically reply, "I came to see you. This is my favorite class, and I didn't want you to miss me." Then he would torture me. Day after day this went on. He was a ringleader naturally. I couldn't write on the board. Every time I turned around, he would throw things at me. Sometimes coins, sometimes pencils, sometimes books—whatever was convenient. I began to master writing on the board facing the class as I wrote sideways. One of his favorite things to do was to come in and declare that he was going to bring in a gun and kill me and everyone in the room. I followed procedures. I wrote him up. I met with the principal. I met with his counselor. The response: "Oh, he's just a kid. He's just letting off steam. Just ignore him." Now, keep in mind this was pre-Columbine.

Billy proved to be too much for his single mother to handle. I not only informed administration of Billy's threats but also called home nearly daily. Teaching 101 dictates that *strong communication between teachers and parents is essential for student well-being and success.* I followed this protocol to the letter. I taught Billy seventh period, and my planning period was eighth period. I spent nearly every eighth period on the phone with Billy's mother. I became her therapist. So, when I would call home and say, "Hi, this is Ms. Klein. Your son threatened to kill me again today." I would be met with a pause and then, gasping for air, she would sob: "I know. He threatened to kill me too."

Needless to say, calling home didn't quite work. Billy continued to torture me. He swore every name you could imagine at me as he threatened me daily. One day, he brought in what he said was itching powder and threw it all over the room. The other students (who also had their own difficulties) started to run around the room, hang out the windows, and scream. I stood in front of the class trying to collect the order of the room. I was trying a different approach that day. I was going to teach my lesson that I prepared no matter what. Dammit. I was introducing *Romeo and Juliet* that day. Period. I managed to get most of the students back into their seats, and I started the lesson. I don't know if I actually got itching powder on me, if it indeed was itching powder, but I started to itch like hell. All over I itched. Deeply, I itched. AGONIZINGLY, I ITCHED. But I wouldn't scratch. I stood there for the remainder of the class uttering bits and pieces about Shakespeare and the Tragedy of Romeo and some chick (*gooooooooood god I wanted to rip my skin off*) Juliet, but I would be damned if I'd let him see me scratch.

This sort of behavior went on for months. Then during one of my eighth-period therapy sessions with the mother, she told me that she was trying to get her son placed in rehab because he had a drug problem. The judge told her that she needed to get evidence from teachers explaining his behavior and how he needed help. Would I write a letter to help her get him placed in rehab? *Would I?* Would I ever. I wrote the letter of all letters. I had a semester's worth of documentation of Billy's behavior, his threats, his definite need for some type of help. I can't remember the length of this letter, but it must've been long. The mother called and thanked me. The letter worked. Billy was sent to rehab. Relief at last. I still had quite a few other issues to deal with in this class, but the ringleader, the scariest one, was gone. Or so I thought. In my naïveté, I assumed that Billy would be out of my class for the rest of the year. I let my guard down.

Then, one day about a month or two later, halfway through class, the door opened. It was Billy. Not escorted by a principal, a counselor, a guard, nobody. Just shows up. "I'm back," he says in this creepy, I'm-going-to-destroy-you-now voice.

Funny thing about schools: you would think that if a volatile student was out of rehab, that maybe just maybe somebody would give the teacher a heads-up that the student was returning to school. Nope. This type of surprise has happened to me and other teachers countless times.

Anyway, the return of Billy. If Billy hated me before I wrote the letter that got him sent to rehab, now he really wanted to kill me. After a brief respite from his torture, he continued to make my life a living hell until the end of the school year. I truly believe that meditating helped me to not quit teaching forever during that year. Here's the thing, meditating didn't remove Billy from my class or magically make the class well behaved, but it did help me to release the tension of each day. When I meditated after school, I was able to let go of the stress of the day of teaching and reduce the tendency to dwell on all of the bad stuff from that day.

I survived that year of Billy. Then I didn't hear anything about him for a number of years. He just sort of vanished. One of the beautiful things about meditation, too, is its ability to help you ruminate less on past stress. So, through meditation, I was able to let the stress of Billy go and the stress of that entire year go. I managed to pretty much completely forget about Billy and the hell he put me through.

Then, one day years later, I was staying late after school grading papers. The students left the building around 2:30 and this was about 4:30. All of the teachers had already left as well. The halls were deserted. I went downstairs to check my mailbox outside of the main office. The office was dark. I put my key into my mailbox, and as I was pulling my mail out, I felt hands clench down upon my shoulders. Then I heard it. I heard the sick, twisted voice I hadn't heard for years. "Ms. Klein. Do you remember me?"

I froze. Without turning around, I knew instantly whom that voice belonged to. Panic filled my body, and I thought, "Here he is. He's come back after all of these years to make good on his promise to kill me." Quickly, I went into survival mode. Left or right? Should I try to break free and run to the left or to the right? What is the closest exit? Where will I have the best chance to find a janitor who can help me?

As I tried to turn, he grabbed me into a tight bear hug. I thought this is it. I was waiting for the knife in my back. I screamed. He spun me around and finally put me down. I started to back away, trying to determine the best strategy to survive. He kept coming closer, and the exchange went something like this:

"Ms. Klein. Do you remember me?"
"Uh, huh. Yeah. I rememmmmmber you."
"Do you remember how I used to throw things at you?"
"Uh, no… no… that was a long time ago." (Of course, I remembered! I just didn't want to trigger any negative thoughts or ideas here for him!)
"Do you remember how I used to threaten to kill you?"
"Uh, … haaa…. I'm sure you didn't mean it." I continued to slowly back away as he kept following. I used as calm a tone as I could. "Hey, Billy, nice to see you. Hope you're doing well. I gotta go." I tried my best to keep things calm and normal and most importantly get away safely.
"Well, I came back to tell you I'm sorry."
"That's nice, Billy… wait, what?" I still didn't trust him.
"Yeah, I was an asshole in your class. I feel bad for doing all of that stuff to you. I wanted to come back and apologize, and I wanted you to know that I've changed."

Billy and I ended up talking for a long time that day. He told me that he eventually went back to rehab, got clean, got his GED, and joined the military. He was a different person. I was overcome with so many emotions during this entire exchange. It was a journey from fear to love for me. Billy became one of my greatest teachers. He taught me to never write off a student. When I had him in class, I thought that Billy would end up dead in a gutter someday or be in jail for putting someone else dead in a gutter.

This was an extremely valuable lesson for me as a teacher. I'm a *Star Wars* fan. Whenever I think about this story of Billy or the other stories of some of my more troubled students, I think of the philosophical advice given by Yoda[1]: "Fear is the path to the dark side. Fear leads to anger. Anger leads to hate. Hate leads to suffering."

The year I taught Billy, I journeyed down this path. I feared Billy. I feared the chaos that he created in the room. I feared his threats. This led me to becoming angry with him and with the circumstances of having him in class. Why did *I* have to be his teacher? Why couldn't he be in *someone else's* class?! It wasn't fair! I hated that class period. I hated having to deal with this student. Ultimately, I suffered during that class period and really most of the day as I dreaded having to deal with this student.

How Meditation Helped

Over time, meditation has continued to help me move from a fear-based mindset to more of a compassion mindset. It has helped me not only to release the stress of challenging students and classroom situations but also to perceive my students with more dignity and understanding. I stopped taking their behavior as personally. I was able to forgive more easily and to more compassionately recognize the person behind the behavior. Inappropriate or dangerous behavior should never be condoned and should never be permitted; however, instead of dismissing the student as a lost cause, I began to develop a compassionate realization that every student has potential and every person has value. Instead of feeding the fire of a particular problem with more fear and anger, I was able to shed light upon it with the opposite force of compassion. Meditation helped to guide me away from the path of fear and led me toward a path of love.

Note

1 Lucas, G. (Director). (1999). *Star wars: episode 1—the phantom menace* (film). Lucasfilm.

9

Surviving a Toxic Workplace

How Meditation Shielded Me from the Negative Effects of Co-Worker Tensions

The Snake Pit

Flashback:

> "It's a snake pit."
>
> "Excuse me?"
>
> "It's a snake pit. And what I want to know is how you are going to handle it? It's a very divided department, and department meetings usually break out in arguments. As a new teacher, how will you deal with that? How will you take a side?"
>
> I just look at the principal and think, "What the heck is he talking about? I haven't even met these people yet."
>
> "I'm sorry. I don't know what I'll do. I guess I'll try to stay neutral."

He chuckles slightly and warns me that the dynamics of the English Department will be challenging to navigate.

I'm confused and disheartened. I was really excited to show him my portfolio and tell him about all of my clever ideas for teaching poetry. This is before the days of electronic portfolios, so perched on my lap is a four-inch, ten-pound, red three-ring binder. I'm just waiting to lift it up onto his desk and open to the perfect examples of my lesson ideas, writing samples, and creative group projects from my student teaching days, letters of recommendation, pictures from my field work in England, and all the other stuff I was told by professors to showcase in job interviews. In an awkward way, I force the subject of my portfolio and do my best to show the principal bits and pieces from my beautifully tabbed and sheet-protected masterpiece. He had zero interest in looking at any of it.

The crux of the interview was determining how I was going to deal with the strife of the department. I wasn't expecting this. Dealing with difficult co-workers was not a chapter in any of the teaching textbooks I read. I don't recall any of my college courses having us read, analyze, and then work in groups to evaluate case studies on fights breaking out in the faculty room. The Praxis exams didn't assess this knowledge.

During my first few weeks as a teacher, a younger English teacher who had taught here for a couple of years took me under her wing. She warned me not to trust ANYONE in the department. She told me not to even fully trust *her* telling me this but that I would soon see for myself. It was better to keep to yourself she cautioned. She advised me to emulate this one male teacher who taught in the department. He never talked to anyone. After decades of teaching here, he managed to remain a complete nonentity. Except for going to the bathroom, he never left his room. He was a recluse. Admired by everyone for being able to sustain an aura of mystery, he was as unassuming as you could be. If he was a color, he'd be beige. Physically and socially he was beige. In fact, he typically wore beige pants, a light-colored shirt with a slightly less light-colored tie every day which blended into his bald, beige head. He didn't even verbally say, "Hi" if he happened to bump into you in the hall on his way to the bathroom. He'd just sort of smile and put up his hand in a wave type of gesture, redirect his eyes to the floor, and continue on quickly. The teacher who taught next door to him for almost 30 years could hardly tell you anything about him. By all accounts, the man was a genius. He came to work every day, left without ever getting mixed up in any of the department drama, and collected his paycheck unscathed. In department meetings, he sat in the back corner or against the wall and just stared down at the desk with his hands folded. He had been on a self-declared silent retreat at work for 30 plus years.

As intriguing an idea as it was to become a female version of this enigmatic man, it was impossible. Nobody else was able to do it, and I was no different. I tried. I tried to not talk to anybody, but that just wasn't realistic. We needed to talk, to collaborate, to discuss ideas. But communicating can be messy, and with so many people in the department with very definite ideas of what and how we should teach, there were bitter exchanges and endless hostilities. English teachers are a special breed. Historically, they are the workhorses of the school. They are the rule followers, the declarers of all that is right and wrong. Of course, they have the wit, the poise, and the vocabulary to shred any opponent in a debate. With their outspoken nature and flair for theatrics, English teachers are the tigers in any school. Diluted in a whole-school environment, the tiger energy balanced out the milder energy of other departments, but concentrated together, the English Department was a force to reckon with, and when the tigers turned on one another, it was wise to take cover. By the way, the younger teacher who first befriended me and warned me of the political hazards of the department ended up quitting two years later.

A Promotion

About nine years into my career, I was promoted to Chair of the English Department. At least I thought it was a promotion. Clearly, I was inheriting a long history of dysfunction and turmoil that the English Department was infamous for. This new position came with a tremendous amount of stress and conflict. The department was composed of about 15 teachers, and it was divided into several factions and endless infighting. Everyone was vying for the best schedule of courses to teach every year, which led to acts of sabotage and betrayal. As chair, I had no administrative authority to do anything concrete to solve these problems. I just became the dumping ground for everyone's complaints.

The irony was that I had developed this lovely balance with my students and was really hitting my stride as a teacher. It was just the adults in my department who were now the thorn in my side. I was a punching bag stuck in the middle of my department and administration. Fellow English teachers whom I used to be good friends with turned on me. One teacher whom I viewed as a mentor and really enjoyed working with and even going out with after school developed a habit of putting her head down during department meetings and groaning loudly as I tried to share information. Another teacher whom I was previously friends with would secretly time every meeting I held, and if I ended the meeting early, she ran and reported me to the office. Seriously. Who is intentionally looking to have longer meetings? But this teacher was a stickler for perfection, and according to the guidelines, we were to have a certain number of meetings that lasted a certain amount of time. The list of these types of petty little action went on and on. That was year 1 of being department chair. I learned to circumvent many of these issues, but the undercurrent of discontent and turmoil continued to linger throughout the department.

One of my favorite pastimes as department chair was having teachers complain about a particular program or procedure that administration implemented. I would share their concerns with the principal, who would then agree to come and meet with the department to discuss whatever the issue was at the time. I would arrange the meeting, the principal would attend, and I would begin the meeting by introducing the topic at hand and discussing an overview of our concerns. Then the principal would ask the department what they thought about the situation, and… nothing. They would sit silently and say nothing, or they would say very little. A few teachers would be courageous enough to share their thoughts, but the majority would sit silently. The principal would look at me like I was crazy; there were no problems here, and that was that. But the department would still be unhappy and continue to complain to me about the issue.

In defense of my department, they weren't necessary wrong in their complaints. I'm not sure if every school overloads their English teachers with additional administrative tasks, but my school certainly did. We were put in charge of countless additional assignments to squeeze into our already-packed schedules. Besides teaching one of only three tested subjects at the high school level in the state-wide exam system (to which teacher evaluations were linked) and having the greatest of amount of work outside of school hours (grading papers, etc.), we were responsible for disseminating nearly every school and district-wide program to the students. For example, we were often in charge of non-English curricular-related things such as health screenings, active shooter response lessons, student scheduling, and countless other paperwork tasks throughout the year that had to be passed out, explained to students, and collected/tracked down by our department. We were rarely given any extra time to accomplish these bonus tasks, and other departments were spared most of these additional responsibilities.

I would express all these concerns in meetings with administration and state the unfairness of the overload of work, suggesting the idea of spreading the wealth of some of these tasks to other departments. The reply usually centered on the logistics of English being the only subject required for all four years of high school, so we were the department that saw all the students every day. But some administrators would offer a more honest explanation and say that they were able to rely the most on the English Department because we always got the job done, correctly, and on time. Whenever I would ask for more time for the department to accomplish everything we needed to because we were already putting in countless hours of overtime in grading essays and papers, some administrators would say, "Well, you should have thought about that before becoming English teachers." One of my favorite responses was "They didn't have to press the 'English teacher' button. You all could've pressed another button when deciding your career." Or the curt dismissive retort, "I hear Wal-Mart is hiring."

But *somebody* needs to teach English, so these cavalier responses were not helpful.

This ping-pong game of being stuck in the middle of administration and my department was never fun. I was in a no-win situation most of the time. I still had a full teaching load, and I had no actual power or authority to make any decisions regarding scheduling, curriculum, programs, or staffing. I could offer suggestions; however, at the end of the day, administration called the shots. But I got blamed by my department for everything. I was administration's scapegoat.

I fell into the trap of trying to control situations and solve everyone's problems. It backfired each time. Whenever someone would come to me complaining about something, I felt it was my duty to fix it. So I would address the problem with the other person(s) it pertained to. Big mistake. I thought that addressing the issues directly with both parties involved was the right thing to do. I was wrong. After many failed attempts, I realized that people really just wanted to vent to me, and the more I inserted myself into a situation, the angrier people became. I also tried to build unity within the department but was unsuccessful. I tried everything from inviting the whole department over to my house for dinner to bringing in breakfasts for everyone and stocking the department planning room with treats. Nothing worked. I eventually realized that I can't control all situations and that I needed to let people fight their own battles.

How Meditation Helped and Didn't Help

I wish that I could say meditation made the conflict within my department better, but it didn't. I still meditated, however, because I could tell a significant difference between the days I meditated and the days I didn't. When I think back, I wonder how I was able to survive in the department chair position for nearly 14 years. Chairs from different departments in the building would witness what I went through and ask me how on earth I could deal with all that stress. I told them I meditated. It didn't necessarily help the problems, but it helped me keep my sanity. It also protected my body from the emotional shrapnel that was flying around my department. And this is quite significant—what

I did notice was that meditation seemed to shield me from the negative effects of this stress on my physical and mental health. I noticed my health and overall well-being were better than those of many of my contemporaries. Some people in my department would get really sick several times a year, necessitating missing a week or more of school at a time. Frequently, these teachers were my age or younger and seemed to be constantly sick with colds, flu, respiratory problems, you name it. A few teachers in my department would use up all their sick days and had to take unpaid days. I really think that it was the amount of stress these teachers were under that caused some of them to get sick so often.

Not to claim that I never got sick, but truly I rarely got really sick. As different illnesses would move their way through my department, either I was spared from them or I seemed to recover faster than many of my fellow teachers. In fact, when I had my first child, I had so many sick days saved up that I was able to take extra maternity leave. I don't have any irrefutable proof that directly connects my practice of meditation with my immune system being stronger, but I really do believe that meditation absolutely enhanced my ability to stay healthier. Maybe it helped me release stress from my body. Maybe I was in a better mental state and felt psychologically better as an effect of meditation. My body appeared to have better resiliency and endurance, even in times of constant stress.

10

Synchronicity

The Bumpy Road that Turned into a Clear Path

While I was teaching full-time, I decided to return to school to complete my doctoral degree in education. Because of my own experiences with teaching and meditating, I wanted to research the effects of meditation on the development of self-actualizing qualities in classroom teachers. When I started the program around 2004, there was very little research on meditation and teaching; I was considered cutting-edge at my university, where some professors believed that the idea of researching meditation was just plain ridiculous. Perhaps I could focus my research on something more mainstream and practical such as reading strategies or evaluation techniques? I almost folded and considered focusing on international education or study abroad programs, which were also subjects I was passionate about, but something kept pulling me back to meditation. I felt that this was the area that could most benefit the future of education. Since 2008, when I defended my dissertation, research and implementation of mindfulness and meditation in schools have skyrocketed.

I remember making an appointment with the professor who was considered the qualitative research guru at my school. He was more non-traditional, and I thought he might be able to tell me for certain if I was crazy or not for wanting to focus on meditation. It seemed that all of the other students in my cohort were selecting topics that were very logic-based and more conventional. I told myself that if this eccentric professor thought my idea was crazy, then I would know I shouldn't pursue it. He would be the litmus. I timidly explained my idea to him, and he liked it. He asked me why I was so hesitant about it. I explained that it's a bit unconventional, and I was worried about it being an acceptable topic for a Catholic university. He laughed. He explained that, of course, this was an excellent topic for a student at this university to focus on because the whole mission of the university revolved around the spirit. He encouraged me to pursue the topic of meditation with courage and confidence.

I had several members of my dissertation committee who were also extremely supportive of my research area; however, I had one professor who couldn't see past the potential religious aspects of meditation. This was really frustrating because even though I was providing the historical, religious, and cultural backgrounds of various traditions of meditation in my literature review, my actual research was focusing on secular meditation. In fact, the focus was largely based on humanistic psychology. In one of our one-on-one meetings in his office, he pounded his fist on his desk and started to scream profanities at me, including "God is a FUCKING ASSHOLE!" The notion of God or his personality was not being argued in my research, so this professor's violent rant was quite out of place. This professor's behavior in general was arrogant and verbally abusive, especially to female students and colleagues. The two female professors on my committee were equally upset about his behavior. Even though the chair of my committee felt that this professor should be removed from my committee, I was told the only way I could remove him was to find and prove that there was another professor who was more qualified to serve on my committee. That was impossible. This professor was a big wig researcher at the university, and I couldn't find any other professor at my university I could prove to be more qualified. He was considered untouchable. This was the end of the spring semester. I needed a miracle if I was going to be able to move forward with my dissertation topic.

I meditated on finding a solution to this problem into the summer months. I was confident that there must be an answer to this dilemma. I made it part of my meditation practice to begin by sitting down quietly with the intention of receiving clarity and guidance. I then would transition into my regular meditation. Later in the summer, my husband and I went to Spain and stayed with friends who lived in Valencia. While visiting our friends, we went in and out of countless churches as we toured different parts of the country. After a while, even though the churches were beautiful and historically interesting, we sort of started to become desensitized to them. One church-touring experience ran into the next. Then, in a cathedral in Barcelona, I stumbled upon an altar to St. Teresa of Avila, an early Christian mystic. I had just finished reading a book about her, and I related my personal struggles with my professor with her struggles as a woman who practiced contemplative prayer (a form of meditation) in a time period when it could have led to severe punishment, including death. This small altar somehow caught my eye in the dimly lit perimeter of the church. I paused to acknowledge the significance of this encounter and decided to light a candle and ask St. Teresa to guide me through this challenge. I'm not necessarily a religious person, but I do believe in the power of the spirit and in the universe providing guidance. I also believed that discovering this altar was not a mere coincidence.

A Synchronistic Connection

I returned home from Spain and resumed my research. About a week after being home, an article connecting meditation with classroom teachers popped up in my search. I had been searching for research on this topic for a couple of years, and neither this article nor the author had ever surfaced. There was scant literature at the time in this area, so I was beyond delighted to find this. It was the perfect piece of support for my topic. At the end of the article appeared the author's name and contact information. His name was Dr. John Miller, and he was a professor and acting chair in the Department of Curriculum, Teaching and Learning at the Ontario Institute for Studies in Education at the University of Toronto. I emailed him and asked for his help. I explained my dissertation topic and asked him if he could suggest any other sources/research that I could examine. I didn't know if he would even receive my email, let alone read and respond to it, but within hours, while he was in Japan, he responded to my inquiry. He referred me to his book. This person literally wrote *the* book on my topic.

I read his book, *The Contemplative Practitioner: Meditation in Education and the Professions*.[1] I realized that there was no doubt that this professor was indeed the expert I was looking for. But would he agree to be on my committee? He was not only from another university, he was in another country (long before the days of Zoom). Toronto is quite the distance from Pittsburgh. But, believing in the power of synchronicity, I reached out to him again. Would he be able/willing to serve on my committee?

He accepted. Here's where it gets chilling. His son had recently moved to Pittsburgh, and this would be a wonderful opportunity to visit him. He would be happy to make the journey down to Pittsburgh. What are the odds? I was filled with amazement. He continued to send me helpful sources to read and apply to my dissertation. I was able to prove that I found a professor who was more qualified to serve on my committee than the hostile professor. The professor from the University of Toronto replaced the other professor and provided a high level of support and guidance for my research. Everything fell into place. My dissertation title was *Developing Higher Consciousness: The Effects of Mantra Meditation on the Development of Self-Actualizing Qualities in Teachers*.[2] I must note here that my dissertation committee was now composed of professors who all embodied these qualities of self-actualization themselves, making them all the ideal people to serve on my committee. Wholeheartedly, I believe that through meditation, I was able to attract the right people at the right time to guide me along my path. This is one of the most magnificent aspects of long-term meditation. The more I meditate, the more I notice these occurrences of synchronicity in my life. These experiences bring about a feeling of being deeply connected with the flow of life and with the majesty and magic of life's unlimited possibilities.

How Meditation Helped

Without a doubt, meditation—and specifically meditating on finding a solution to my dissertation committee—provided me with the guidance and clarity I needed. Here's why. By meditating, I was able to let go of the stress and anxiety that were natural responses to the professor who came at me with such anger and hostility. When I left his office that day, I made it halfway down the hallway before I broke down in tears. I felt like someone punched me in the gut. I felt vulnerable, defeated, sad, confused, and hopeless. I could have succumbed to these feelings and just given up. Completion rates for doctoral programs were less than 50% nationally, we were told. I could have changed topics, left the program as ABD (All BUT Dissertation), or postponed my studies, wallowing in anger and insecurity. Rather, I decided to meditate on a different option. The first thing that the process of meditating allowed me to do was to release the stress of these encounters faster than I would have been able to otherwise. These negative emotions did not fester in me and lodge themselves in my body and my mind. Meditating helped me to soften them and ultimately relinquish them.

Second, meditation shifted my focus from dwelling on the problem to focusing on finding a positive and beneficial solution. Instead of just wading in the self-pity quagmire of "poor me I have a mean professor, I'm in a no-win situation, and I should just give up now," I was able to shift to a more positive mindset and *know* that there was an answer out there that would not only resolve the problem I was having but actually prove this difficulty was a blessing in disguise. Because of meditation, I didn't become the victim of the situation; I became the beneficiary of it.

Third, meditation helped to calm my mind, which fostered a mode of receptivity. I was able to notice and be aware of possibilities when they showed up. Meditation facilitated my ability to be alert and open to receiving answers, guidance, and solutions that I was previously unable to imagine. This is one of the most profound effects of long-term meditation. The frequency of my experiences of synchronicity has increased the longer I've meditated. I believe this is due to my mind being calmer and more open to higher states of awareness through years of training in meditation.

Notes

1 Miller, J. P. (1994). *The contemplative practitioner: Meditation in education and the professions.* Toronto: The Ontario Institute for Studies in Education Press.
2 Klein, L. (2008). *Developing higher consciousness: The effects of mantra meditation on the development of self-actualizing qualities in teachers.* Pittsburgh, PA: Duquesne University.

11

Training for the Worst

The Watershed of Terror

On April 20, 1999, two years into my teaching career, the tragedy of the Columbine High School mass shooting occurred. Unless you were a teacher in the United States before Columbine and in the years to follow Columbine, I don't think you can fully comprehend just how much this event profoundly and permanently altered our education system and how much it exacerbated the underlying stress and anxieties experienced by both teachers and students. As I described in Chapter 8, the student who used to come in my room nearly every day and threaten to shoot me and shoot everyone in the room wasn't taken seriously since it was before Columbine and such an atrocity was still inconceivable.

It would be comforting if I could say the Columbine tragedy was a fluke event; however, since Columbine, there have been many other mass shootings in U.S. schools.[1] Owing to the ongoing occurrences of school violence, teachers, administrators, and students have entered a whole new instructional paradigm: surviving an active shooter.

Pre-Columbine, students would make threats, and most people (at least most people I encountered) didn't take it very seriously. Then bam! In one horrible, unprecedented day, the climate of the American school system altered in unimaginable ways both physically and psychologically. I had moved to New York

City with my husband for a year and was teaching in one of the boroughs of the city at the time of Columbine. I was hired by an outside agency who had a contract with the school. The school already had four other teachers quit that year for that particular position because the students were so badly behaved. It was a rough teaching placement to say the least. In the aftermath of Columbine, students barricaded me in my room and physically threatened me. My classroom was isolated in the basement of the building and didn't have cell reception, so it was quite frightening. With the tragedy of Columbine, my already palpable fears for my safety accelerated to acute levels and led to my resignation from that school. However, the schools that people most fear, the inner-city schools that have the most overtly troubled, low-achieving students, are not the typical environments for Columbine type of horrors. Time and again, it's the picturesque suburban school setting that becomes the host of such atrocities.

Meet A.L.I.C.E.

You're going to need to wear long sleeves and running shoes.

Those were the instructions that teachers were given leading up to our in-service training at the start of the school year. Now, in the middle of my teaching career, with the increased number of school shootings across the country, schools were starting to conduct active-shooter drills. If you have been a student or a teacher in school in the U.S. in the past two decades, you have undoubtedly been through what I'm describing here. In our school district and in other districts around the country, a system called A.L.I.C.E. was being implemented.[2] A.L.I.C.E. stands for alert, lockdown, inform, counter, and evacuate. This program was being utilized to increase the chance of survival during a school shooting. Previously, teachers and students were taught to hide in the classroom, try to lock/barricade the door, and squat quietly in a back corner of the room. The problem? Everyone became sitting ducks.

So, with A.L.I.C.E., you didn't necessarily lock down. A.L.I.C.E. provided training in options to use in lieu of lockdown when possible or in addition to locking down. We were trained in alternate techniques such as counterattacking with whatever objects we had near us: scissors, books, paperweights. We practiced using a belt to tether the door in a more secure way. All of which, really, were laughable defenses against semi-automatic weapons. But, still, we as teachers strategized and were told we were allowed to bring in anything (except guns and knives) that we could possibly use as weapons to keep in our classrooms. I opted for a wooden club and cans of wasp spray that shot 20 feet. I heard of some teachers bringing in buckets of rocks to keep under their desk. Some teachers brought in baseball bats and stored them in the closets of their rooms. We set to work to determine what the best objects were that we could weaponize in case of the unimaginable.

We were trained in how to best evacuate. Was the risk of jumping out a window better than a bullet? I was on the third floor, way too high, so I was either locking down and counterattacking or trying to evacuate by another means. I grappled with this dilemma: if I was by myself, I had mapped out several possible escape routes and hiding places along the way for safe passage, but if I had 30 students with me, forget it. No way we could move a body of people that fast through the halls and stairwells—while most likely bottlenecking with other classes. No, I had tried to work that out in my head many times. Each time, I saw us being trapped in a stairwell—sitting ducks. If you have ever participated in a whole-school fire drill, you can appreciate that moving large groups of students out, quickly, inconspicuously, without jamming up hallways and stairwells isn't so easy. Add the chaos of an active shooter to the mix, and you'll realize the option of evacuation for an entire class on the top floor of a building isn't as simple as it sounds.

It became a habit of mine to run through evacuation strategies and hiding places everywhere I was in the building. If I had my students in the library, I imagined how we could best barricade the doors and maybe climb out the window onto the flat roof. But then what? Too high to jump off of the roof, so now we were just sitting ducks potentially on the rooftop. If I was in the faculty restroom, I could lock the door. Maybe I could climb up onto the sink and lift myself into the rafters? But could it hold my weight? If I was in the hallway, near the center of the building, maybe I could hide in the book room. More open spaces like the cafeteria seemed most problematic for hiding. It was surrounded with entry points and windows. The only hope was to somehow be able to flee, maybe counterattack.

These worst-case scenario drills became the undercurrent of my mind wherever I was in the building. Of course, there was no possible way to completely plan for an active shooter. There are countless variables, and everything can shift very quickly in such a fluid situation. Still, somehow silently rehearsing different scenarios in my mind gave me a sense of calm as I felt that I was at least theoretically more prepared. Being taught that there are different options for survival is one thing, but actually considering each option and weighing the pros and cons of different options at various points throughout the building allowed me to realize that teachers and students needed to be aware of their surroundings at all times.

I don't know if other teachers did this mental exercise on a regular basis like I did. I never told anyone about it, so maybe other teachers did this type of thing as well and just never talked about it either. I am consciously aware that I may sound paranoid admitting all of this. With every news report of the latest school shooting, however, I think it does awaken a sense of necessity in being alert and always prepared.

Getting back to the active-shooter training drill for teachers, the district brought in people who were equipped with weapons to actually shoot at us. It was a live simulation drill in which we were dispersed around the school, and it was go-time with active shooters coming at us with pellet guns. We were being shot at. We could do whatever we had to do to try to survive. We were separated into "classes." First, we had to try the lockdown simulation, and I found myself in a room with a group of other teachers. We tethered and barricaded the door with whatever we happened to have. It felt frighteningly realistic. I went into complete survival mode, totally in the present moment, and oddly developed a strength I never realized I had, being able to move large pieces of furniture across the room with lightning speed.

One teacher even commented that she didn't realize I was so strong—neither did I. I had one goal: Don't get shot! Pellet guns might not kill you, but they sure as hell hurt. The entire scene during the training drill was quite chaotic, and several teachers sustained injuries.

Naturally, the English Department was put in charge of training the student body on A.L.I.C.E. Every student in the building had an English class, so that was how they ensured training across the school. Instead of conducting live drills with students, we presented information via PowerPoint and had discussions. It gave students more options for saving themselves. As teachers, we had to watch the footage of Columbine. It haunts me to this day. We had to analyze how more people could have survived. In one instance, there were a couple of students who wanted to run out of the room they were in—I believe it was the library, but the staff member there told them they had to stay there hiding. They were killed. Running could have led to their escape and could have saved them. Now, students are taught to do whatever they need to do to increase their chance of survival—no permission from a teacher is needed.

Also, if a student is out in the hall and an active-shooter alert is signaled, that's it. If the class goes into lockdown, that door doesn't open for any reason. That student could be banging on the door and pleading to enter, and we are instructed to never jeopardize the rest of the class for one student. So I instructed my students to individually hide and get out of the building in any way they could if they were in a hallway. Never bother returning to a classroom. Run out (with your hands up in the air if there were police there) and run out into the adjacent neighborhoods and hide somewhere. These were difficult lessons to teach students. You could feel their anxiety and fear and sense of helplessness.

We had other training workshops as well in the event of mass casualties. In some of these workshops, we were trained to administer torniquets and stuff gunshot wounds with whatever we had available—tampons were quite useful for this. The idea of all these trainings was to increase survivability. I was watching the news after the school shooting that occurred in

Nashville in March 2023. The person who had previously conducted active-shooter training with the teachers and staff at that school was interviewed. He said that the teachers did implement the training and successfully barricaded their classrooms, which saved many lives. According to this person being interviewed, the victims were mainly in open spaces such as hallways when they encountered the shooter. So training teachers and students does work. It can minimize fatalities, but there is no guarantee of being able to safeguard everyone.

Obviously, being prepared is a good thing; however, with each of these training sessions, there came an added level of fear and feelings of dread. Some of the building staff made jokes about it as a coping mechanism. One of the administrative assistants nervously laughed that she would be the first to be shot because her desk was in the open entrance way. Other teachers asserted that we should be allowed to be armed with guns to defend ourselves and our students. We all had our own ways of trying to cope with this undercurrent of fear.

How Meditation Helped

First, I'm going to state the obvious: we must work on multiple levels to address the issues of school violence. We must work to take action to safeguard our schools. Real reforms need to be put into place to help protect schools—and all spaces—from such horrors at national and state levels. Each school must continue to be vigilant training students and teachers in what to do in the event of an active shooter and must have safety protocols, including having secure buildings. As a country, we must address mental health issues. The urgency of taking these measures cannot be stressed enough.

As we are working to take action to prevent school violence, we need to have ways for teachers (and students) to cope with the stress and anxiety created by the very thought of it. Terror is not just actually going through a violent situation; terror is also created by the everyday threat that something bad could happen. This everyday, perpetual fear experienced by students and teachers takes a toll on one's mental health. Living in fear and uncertainty, which is exacerbated by other events such as the Covid pandemic, can instill feelings of hopelessness, dread, and anger in people. These emotions can have a devastating impact upon somebody's mental and physical well-being and can even be felt throughout the entire environment of the building.

Meditating was how I personally survived the stress of this new paradigm of education. I found myself meditating more at school. I meditated during my lunch period and sometimes during my planning period. I would shut my classroom door and sit at my desk to meditate for 20 minutes. By meditating during my lunch period, I had a resurgence in my energy levels while having a feeling of calmness and presence. In the class periods that followed my meditation, I felt more present for my students.

But here's the really interesting outcome: my students could sense the energy of the room. They would enter from a chaotic hall scene, and I would hear them say things to each other, and sometimes directly to me, that they were so happy to be in my room. This was their favorite classroom. They didn't know why, but they really liked this space. It felt warm and welcoming. They would even compare it with other classrooms that they said felt colder, harsher, not as welcoming. More than ever, my goal became to create a sanctuary for my students. Meditating has the ability to not only affect the meditator but also the space around the meditator. It's subtle. Meditating, especially in the same place over time, will begin to alter the vibrational quality of the room. I couldn't protect my students from all the dangers of the world, but I wanted them to experience a sense of tranquility and take a pause from the harshness of life, even if just for a class period.

Notes

1 The Associated Press. March 27, 2023. https://apnews.com/article/nashville-mass-school-shooting-database-columbine-uvalde-1c82749f7236752a2e621f402489b357

2 https://www.alicetraining.com/

12

Dr. Mom, the Vampire

The Vampire

"Okay, what are you laughing at?"

Several students exchange looks and then start to mumble. I've learned long ago not to take things personally as a teacher. Every day, I have about 150 sets of teenage eyes critiquing me. I figured I must have part of my lunch in my teeth or something.

A brave student in the front, center seat of the room finally responds, "We call you a vampire. That's your nickname."

I just look at him. Another student quickly follows, "It's a good thing. You don't age. There's no way you can be as old as you are. We know how long you've taught here, but there's no way you can be that old. That's why we joke you must be a vampire."

Well, I'm not a vampire. And I have absolutely aged. Unfortunately, I notice the fine lines around my eyes when I smile and the "wisdom highlights" that have popped up around my temples—an easy fix to cover, thankfully. So, yes, like every living being, I've aged. However, I do feel that I've aged less and more slowly than many people my age. Others have commented that I look young for my age. A fellow English teacher declared with a literary allusion, "I'm sure there must be a painting of you in your attic!"

I've been asked many times: what do I do to stay youthful, what products do I use on my face, what do I eat? My answer: I meditate. I tell them that I use a good sunscreen and moisturizer and try to eat healthy, too, but really the number one thing I attribute to staying younger longer is meditation. The reason is quite simple. Meditation helps to release stress from the body and mind. Stress ages you. Find ways to cope with stress better, and you'll begin to age more gracefully. Figure 12.1 shows the picture of me taken for the school yearbook at the start of my teaching career, and Figure 12.2 shows the picture of me taken 24 years later after my career as an English teacher. I believe that meditation shielded me from the accelerated aging that stress can cause.

I can literally feel, on a physical level, the stress drop from my body when I meditate.

One of my favorite times to meditate is around 4 p.m., right after school; my body actually craves a meditation at this time. I have an antique fainting couch in my office at home, and this is where I would meditate every day after school. I found that meditating in the same space/seat creates a sort of muscle memory, which allows my body to instantly relax and feel comfortable right from the moment of sitting in this space. I transition into the meditation with greater ease. As I begin meditating, I feel my entire body relax even more, even feeling a surge move through my body that gives me both a sense of release and a soothing sensation.

Consistently releasing stress from the body on a regular basis helps to safeguard the body from the aging effects that tension can cause overtime. I have found that systematically releasing stress from the body through meditation helps my body in the healing and rejuvenation process. I don't think it's any secret that people who are under extreme amounts of stress can show accelerated signs of aging. I've known family and friends who have experienced unrelenting stress from their jobs and who, from being caregivers, begin to literally fall apart physically. Nobody gets out of life without having stress to contend with, but the better somebody can release that stress as quickly as possible, the less harm it will have on the body. I think of it as playing hot potato. You're sitting in the circle (life), and you know that the hot potato (stress) is going to come to you. When it does, do you want to hold onto that hot potato? No. You want to get rid of it as fast as you can!

FIGURE 12.1 Yearbook photo of author taken in 1997, during her first year of teaching

FIGURE 12.2 Photo of author taken in 2021
Photograph by Becky Thurner Braddock.

Dr. Mom

Vampire, thankfully, was not the only name I was called. Some students called me Dr. Mom. This one makes me smile and is what I consider one of my greatest accomplishments as a teacher. A group of students named me this because they said I really cared about them like I would care for my own children. One example: Every year I would take a group of students to New York City for arts and theater immersion opportunities, and during one of the last trips I chaperoned, a girl was found with drugs in her possession. It was a legal issue and also a school violation. More than being angry with the student, I felt extremely sad for her. She was only a sophomore at the time, and I knew that something like this could really ruin her life. After another chaperone and I had to notify the police, her mother, and the principal, the student threatened suicide. Sitting in a straight-back chair that propped the room door open so that I was in the hallway and still able to keep an eye on her, I stayed up all night talking with her and making sure she was safe until our return trip home. Here is an excerpt of the note she sent me afterwards:

> I would like to thank you for being so thoughtful and caring throughout the whole process... I appreciate all the sacrifices you made to make sure I was safe and the helpful advice you gave me when I was feeling helpless. Your advice has made me realize that I can turn myself around from this point and make myself better than I was before. I have learned that I have so much to look forward to and too much to lose to go down that dangerous path.

The Energy We Carry

I developed a compassion and love for my students, and I also truly loved teaching. I loved it not because it was easy or externally rewarding. Rather, I loved it on a deeper level, a level of feeling fulfilled, content, and blissful. This is a feeling that emerged more in the later years of my career. I didn't feel this way all the time. But, in the later years of teaching, this feeling became more frequent and enduring.

I remember walking into the building, pulling my bags loaded with papers and books behind me, and feeling a sense of euphoria. I'm not a morning person, and we had to report by 7 a.m. each day. I knew I had a long day of teaching ahead of me, yet I would feel a sense of blissfulness and lightness as I made the journey from my car across the parking lot, through the halls of the building to my classroom. I could feel this on an emotional and physical level. I experienced a sense of contentment and joy and at the same time a sense of appreciation for being able to teach. Sometimes it would quickly be wiped away by a colleague who would bombard me with complaints upon my unlocking my classroom door. Sometimes it would last throughout my morning classes. Sometimes, if I meditated during lunch, I was able to reconnect with this feeling of bliss. And then there were days when I didn't feel blissful or content at all. Or there were times when I would be teaching a piece of literature, and I would reconnect with this feeling of joy—not just joy in a happy, having-fun sense but in a way in which there was a space around me and around my students, a serene sense of space around the actual moment, a pause in time. This wasn't necessarily a feeling I could manufacture at will. This feeling of bliss came of its own accord, although I found I could create the conditions for it to arise. When I meditated regularly and allowed myself to be in the moment, there was an increase in the likelihood of being able to feel blissfulness and contentment. There were still times when I felt despair or anxiety, but increasingly, in the latter part of my career, I experienced these moments of profound inner peace and happiness.

Students could sense this peace and joy in me as well. I received a message from a student who graduated and whom I didn't even have in class but who knew me:

> "I may not have been your student… but I could feel the energy you brought throughout the high school".

I believe this energy the student is referring to was that feeling of bliss I experienced, and it affected my surroundings. I think this is what is sometimes referred to as "holding the space" that is so important for being a teacher—whether it's a teacher of meditation or of English. We are responsible for the energy that we generate and bring to our space. This applies to our home, our workplace, shops and restaurants, our cars—everyplace we are. We can decide what kind of energy we bring with us, and our energy absolutely affects the space and people around us.

People will pick up on someone's energy. Even dogs can do this. Students are keenly aware of the energy of their teachers. I always think about this one teacher in my school who was extremely good-looking. But his personality didn't match his looks. We were hired around the same time, and I remember trying to say hello to him as we crossed paths in the hallway. We were the only two people in the hall at the time, and it seemed very natural for me to say hello. He just grunted back. Literally, he grunted. He always looked angry. Even though he was a young, good-looking teacher, I would overhear students saying, "Mr. — hates life. He's always miserable." As the years went on, he began to show signs of aging that surpassed his chronological age. He was the perfect example of how one's energy can affect both the person's body and their space. I believe that his negative energy contributed to his accelerated aging and to how students perceived him.

How Meditation Helped

Meditating has enabled me to age at a slower rate and to have a better disposition that permeates my surroundings. Physically and mentally, I feel lighter, happier, and more vibrant. How do I know that meditation has played a significant factor in the way I look and feel? Because, if I get really busy and I miss meditating for a few days, I can see the difference. I will begin to feel more tired, more agitated, and grumpier or have a sense of "blah" about me. I definitely don't feel as vibrant and calm when I miss meditating over a prolonged period of time.

Meditation also prevented me from experiencing burnout, which is a common problem in teachers. I have to say that in all of the years I taught, I never experienced the state of being burned out. I experienced a great deal of stress at times and felt overwhelmed with the workload at times, but I was always passionate about teaching. I was able to maintain my enthusiasm and love for teaching until the end.

In terms of how I perceive others, meditation has given me the gift of being able to be more understanding and compassionate. The longer I have been practicing meditation, the greater this element of compassion for others has grown. Here's a quick story that happened recently. My friend called me up half laughing and half angry about some other mother who lives in a neighboring district. Apparently, this mother's teenage son got into some kind of fight with a group of kids. The mother drove up to wherever these other boys were in some parking lot and started to scream at them and then in her crazed state crashed her car into something. Nobody was harmed. But everyone who heard about it was either laughing at her ridiculous behavior or judging her for being out of control.

As my friend was telling me this story, I felt deep down within me a pit of sadness for this mother. Yes, what she did was stupid, wrong, inappropriate, and dangerous. But I still felt this tremendous welling up of sadness and compassion for her. Anyone who is a mother (or father) might be able to appreciate where this woman had to be emotionally in order for her to do this. In hearing this story, I instantly perceived her pain and suffering. I surrounded this person whom I have never met with love. In my mind, I sent this mother and everyone involved in this situation love and healing. She didn't need my judgment. On a physical level, I felt her sadness, her fear. This is what meditating does. You begin to be able to sense how others, perfect strangers even, are feeling. A simultaneous understanding and compassion arise that present a more objective perspective.

I must have gone silent on the phone as I was sending healing to this mother because my friend paused and asked what I was thinking. *Didn't I think that was awful!? How could this mother be so insane?!* I told her that this mother must have been so scared for her son and wasn't rationally thinking. Yes, she needed to be held accountable for her actions, but she needed kindness and compassion too. My friend laughed at me and told me that my meditating must really be working!

13

A Call to Action that Was Guided by Synchronicity

The Last Few Years of Teaching

As I was feeling more and more a sense of contentment, I noticed that those around me were feeling greater anxiety, agitation, hostility, and depression. Both my fellow teachers and my students expressed feeling extremely anxious and stressed. Consequently, I started to discuss meditation with my students and colleagues more. I started to give presentations on meditation and mindfulness during professional development days to teachers and staff from all the schools in the district. For my students, I found ways to incorporate mindfulness techniques into my lessons, even though it wasn't in the curriculum.

Then I created a semester course for seniors called "Literature of Self-Discovery" in which we read fiction and nonfiction selections that addressed various philosophical issues, including one's purpose in life, the pursuit of happiness, overcoming obstacles, the transcendence of fear, and tapping into one's full potential. Students read fiction and nonfiction texts, including *Siddhartha* by Hermann Hesse, *The Alchemist* by Paulo Coelho, and *Man's Search for Meaning* by Viktor Frankl. Students of all ability levels were open and receptive to exploring these topics and expressed a yearning to delve deeper into topics related to personal improvement, including mindfulness. I started "Mindfulness Mondays" when we would spend the first part of the class period learning and practicing a mindfulness technique. Sometimes I would make hot tea and bring in scones or another type of pastry for everyone to enjoy on those days. This helped the students to center themselves at the start of each week, and they could practice the technique on their own the rest of the week.

Parents were supportive of this new course. Here's an excerpt of one of the emails I received from a parent:

> I wanted to let you know that after only a couple of days, you have changed my daughter's outlook entirely. She came home so excited to tell me about your class and how wonderful you are. She became so positive and is already demonstrating a whole new mindset. She came home and said, 'Mom, I just started this awesome new class and you need to help me get stuff for a vision board!' She proceeded to show me the syllabus… we talked for almost two hours… you've struck a chord in her and I can't thank you enough for teaching such a critically important class…

Another parent wrote to me,

> We would like to thank you for your powerful words of encouragement to our daughter, Alyssa. Your interest makes a profound difference in the way she sees herself and the possibilities for her future….
>
> We so appreciate the positive example you reflect to students. Alyssa and many students and families observe and admire your positivity, drive, comfort with being and expressing yourself, willingness to take risks, and sense of humor and proportion. You model so many aspects of being a healthy adult—kind person, partner, parent, mentor, active learner, professional…. Students observe and learn from you each day. All of this is teaching at its best.

Even before I started this new literature course, I always found it inspiring how receptive and engrossed students were in exploring topics that were related to self-reflection, self-improvement, and self-empowerment. They would come to life every time we analyzed metaphysical aspects of literature and discovered personal connections to what we were reading. Years before I introduced the concept of mindfulness to my students or created the "Literature of Self-Discovery" course, I taught J.R.R. Tolkien to my regular Senior English students. The reading level of Tolkien is easy for the typical student to grasp, but when we would peel back the layers of his work and really dive into the philosophical nature of his writing, students became energized. There was one lecture that I gave on *The Hobbit* that intertwined the literature with students' current state of being seniors in high school, to the nature of life, and to philosophy. It was literary, personal, and uplifting. Every time I gave this talk, the students would applaud. Seriously. I was always shocked. But, every year, in every class that I presented this inspirational talk about the book, students wholeheartedly applauded. I have found that students of all ability levels are keenly interested and receptive to discourse that focuses on hope, possibilities, and awakening to the fullness of themselves. As a teacher, I just needed to help them realize that there's more to life than meets the eye.

At the end of every school year, I would give my farewell speech to every class. In this speech, I recounted our year together, and I went around the room and said something special and personal about each student in the room. These personalized anecdotes were funny, sad, poignant, praising, and reflective, and all had the tone of appreciation in them. I wanted *all* of my students to see that whether or not they had a "good" year in the class, I valued each of them for their own uniqueness. I saw each of them as pure potential who had beautiful journeys ahead of them.

I Needed to Learn More

Of course, not every student was as positive about my teaching. In one class, as I was talking about mindfulness, a girl came up to me and said, "This is really pissing me off." I discovered that this student had a history of trauma, and I realized that I needed to learn more about how to bring mindfulness to an adolescent audience and how to best approach mindfulness if someone has experienced trauma.

I also began to realize that even though I loved teaching literature and writing, there was something more crucial for me to be doing. In observing the high levels of anxiety and depression in my students and my colleagues, I began to shift my purpose, and I developed a keen sense that I needed to be teaching meditation full time. The type of meditation that I practiced and taught for years is designed to be taught one-on-one, and the student must be at least 18 years old, so I wanted to be trained in techniques that allowed me to conduct group sessions with different age levels. I also wanted to complete a master's degree program that would bring credibility to my endeavors.

I found various certification programs for mindfulness here in the States, but I wasn't finding a full master's degree program that was specific to my interests. I decided to cast my net a bit farther afield and began looking at universities around the world that offered a master's degree program in mindfulness. Then, during one of my online searches, I stumbled across the University of Aberdeen's Master of Science program in Mindfulness Studies. The university is located in northern Scotland. I knew nothing about the University of Aberdeen other than the internet telling me it's the fifth oldest university in the United Kingdom, founded in 1495. I asked a friend of mine who lives in England what he knew of Aberdeen or the university, and all he said was "It's cold."

After reviewing the information about the program and realizing that this was exactly what I've been searching for, I applied and waited. A long time went by, and I didn't hear anything. I figured that I must not have gotten in, and believing in the notion that everything happens for a reason, I made my peace with that. It was a hybrid program, so I would be in Scotland several times throughout the year and continue with coursework and research online at home. I also began to realize that if I did get accepted into this program, it wouldn't be feasible for me to complete a program abroad, even if just several times a year, while I still had to work full time. I even began to question the idea of leaving my job to start a new career. Doubt began to creep in. I was at the top of the pay scale, had excellent benefits and a retirement plan, and unmatched job security. If I just taught about ten more years, I would have full retirement and excellent benefits for the rest of my life; I could live very comfortably and never have to work a day ever again. Walking away from my career now didn't seem financially sound. Still, I meditated on it. In my meditations, I focused my intentions on allowing the results to be whatever was meant to be for me and, if I *did* get accepted to the university, finding a financial solution to being able to participate in the program. I concentrated on a clear path being shown to me, so that whatever was meant to be would emerge unambiguously.

Synchronicity Strikes Again

My answer arrived. I received the acceptance email from the University of Aberdeen. Then, out of nowhere, soon after I received the acceptance notification from Aberdeen, the superintendent of my school district sent out an early retirement incentive to teachers that was unprecedented. After declaring the previous year that there would not be another early retirement incentive for at least five years, the district was offering one again this year, and they were doubling the amount of the offer. Unheard of. Truly. Everyone was shocked. Once again, I felt the power of synchronicity at a crucial time in my life. I would now be able to retire early with an additional payout to me. I remember a chill going through my body and looking up at the sky, uttering "Thank you." There was my answer. Now I could financially justify starting anew.

But I still wanted to teach one more year to better budget for this transition and to accrue an additional year for my state pension. Miraculously, the district then added a clause to the retirement agreement that said one could retire at the end of the 2019 *or* the 2020 school year. So far so good, but if I worked one more year, I would need to be able to go over to Scotland a couple of times during that school year. We had only three personal days. That obviously wouldn't cover the time I needed off. I arranged a meeting with the superintendent of my school district. I explained my situation to him and showed him the curriculum of the master's program and what my future career plans were. He was extremely supportive and encouraging. He recognized the importance of studying mindfulness in order to bring it into schools to help both teachers and students. Not only was my superintendent understanding, he was also willing to give me unpaid time off to go over to Scotland to study a couple of times during my final year of teaching. Everything fell into place again. I was and still am extremely grateful.

How Meditation Helped

Meditating enhanced my ability to be aware of not only my needs but also the needs of those around me. I sensed how my students and colleagues were feeling and developed a compassion for them. In wanting to help them, I began to shift my focus. I became more open and receptive to different avenues of teaching. It would have certainly been easier for me to stay on the career path I was on. I would be even closer to retirement now. I could still be teaching English and leaving at the end of each day knowing that I had wonderful job security and contentment. I was definitely in my comfort zone as a teacher. Meditation gave me the courage and insight to see new possibilities for my future, to continue to learn and grow, and to take risks.

As I describe in Chapter 10, meditation created the conditions of a calm, clear mind so that I could be more open and receptive to answers provided through synchronicity that guided me in my decision to leave the classroom. I might not be able to prove that the occurrence of synchronicity was a direct outcome of meditating, but I can confidently say that my awareness and faith in accepting this guidance were definitely a result of meditating.

14

Reflections on My Career and Meditation

Having the Edge

As I reflect on the course of my career, I see the patterns of how meditation empowered me not only to survive but to thrive as a teacher for over 20 years. Meditation shielded me from burnout, has positively affected my physical and mental health, improved my ability to handle stress and conflict, and enhanced my state of being over the course of two decades. I know that meditation has been instrumental in these areas because I could always tell a marked difference in how I felt and functioned when I didn't meditate on a regular basis. Meditation has given me the mental and physical edge to be the healthiest, most youthful, most creative, most insightful, and happiest version of myself in and out of the classroom.

Reflective Analysis of the Early Years

In my early years of teaching, two of the main effects of meditation that were most pronounced for me involved increasing my creativity and problem-solving skills. Whenever an idea came to me through meditation, I noticed that it was almost always a good idea, and it usually always turned out well. There were feelings of positivity and vibrancy to the ideas that came to me. Why did this happen? One of the reasons may be linked to the increase in self-actualizing tendencies, which include creativity and problem-solving abilities. Being in a more relaxed state, I became open and receptive to creativity and new ideas. Even though the concepts of creativity and mindfulness are both difficult to articulate, there is a connection between the practice of meditation and creativity, which can lead to positive effects in the classroom.[1] Another explanation for creativity being fostered through meditation is due to a reduction of fear.[2] The ideas that emanated out of my meditations were authentically free of the fear of being judged. Ideas that emerged in meditation were unencumbered by my doubts.

Another area most notably affected by my meditation practice was my ability to handle stress and conflict more positively in the classroom and, ultimately, to be less reactive. In reflecting upon my teaching experience, I perceive how meditation cultivated my ability to respond, rather than react, to students. Consequently, I was able to shift from fear to love/acceptance/understanding of my students and be more forgiving and less judgmental.

Meditation enabled me to be more creative, less reactive, and more understanding. Although there were times when I still reacted with fear and anger or when I struggled with trying to connect with a student, more positive qualities of compassion and understanding emerged early on in my teaching career and continued to grow throughout my career. When I think back to former students like Dillon, I realize that meditation helped to alleviate my initial fears of them, resulting in greater compassion for them. I believe that practicing meditation buffered me from the stress of teaching and enabled me to be more resilient while becoming a more compassionate, innovative teacher.

Reflective Analysis of the Middle Years

The stress of teaching continued into the middle years of my career, but the type of stress changed. It was more centered on the adults I worked with and on larger-scale fears of school violence. Admittedly, meditation did nothing to help me to solve the problems of animosity in my department. However, I do believe that it helped me to stay physically and mentally healthier. I honestly don't think I could have survived being the chair of the English Department and maintained my health and well-being if it wasn't for meditation.

Meditating helped me to release stress from my body, aiding my ability to stay physically healthy. It also helped me to emotionally heal from stressful encounters by training my mind to focus more on the positive and to avoid ruminating over negative experiences. Meditation helped me to find a sense of calm and balance in the wake of a challenging situation, and I was able to let go of the negativity and stress and move on faster.

By meditating in my classroom, I instilled a sense of calm and peace in my room. As students were encountering more and more reasons to feel anxious with issues such as school violence, I managed to create a welcoming and soothing space for students to be each day. Part of it might have been my teaching, but I believe that a significant contributor to the feeling of safety and peace came from meditating in the room. I don't have any way of proving this, of course, but I think it relates to the notion of "emotional contagion" that is spread from teacher to students.[3] Students are keen to pick up on the emotions of their teachers, and as a teacher, I wanted to serve as a role model for being positive. Sometimes I did this overtly through my words and actions, and sometimes I achieved this simply by holding a space of peace in the room.

Beyond helping me to manage various levels of stress, meditation enabled me to be open to and aware of experiences of synchronicity. These synchronistic events directed me to solutions that emerged from seemingly unlikely coincidences. As described by Carl Jung, these coincidences seemed so improbable that they gave me a felt sense of profound meaning.[4] I was more open to these experiences of synchronicity the more regularly I practiced meditation.

Reflective Analysis of the Later Years

In reflecting upon my later years of teaching, I notice the long-term effects of meditation on my aging and my state of being.

My experience of aging at a slower rate supports the research conducted on telomere length by Blackburn and Epel.[5] More specifically, my experience supports studies suggesting that the effects of meditation on telomere length are dependent upon length of time of practice, and for significant changes in telomere length to occur, long-term meditation practice is required.[6] Having practiced meditation for several decades, I believe that meditation has played a part in my ability to age at a slower rate. There certainly may be other factors such as my diet and skin care; however, I feel that meditation has been a significant contributor.

In considering higher states of awareness associated with long-term meditation, I find evidence in support of this in the feedback I've received from parents and students. I also felt more bliss and contentment both in and out of the classroom. As part of this higher state of awareness, I continued to experience more cases of synchronicity in my later years of teaching. The unfolding of events that led to my transition out of teaching English to embark on a new journey to study mindfulness mirrors Jung's definition of synchronicity: "a coincidence in time of two or more causally unrelated events which have the same or similar meaning."[7] Indeed, I believe that the events ushering me onto a new career path are the very types of coincidence described by Jung as being "connected so meaningfully that their 'chance' concurrence would represent a degree of improbability."[8]

Notes

1 Henriksen, D., Richardson, C., & Shack, K. (2020). Mindfulness and creativity: Implications for thinking and learning. *Thinking Skills and Creativity, 37*, 100689. https://doi.org/10.1016/j.tsc.2020.100689

2 Ibid.

3 Becker, E. S., Goetz, T., Morger, V., & Ranellucci, J. (2014). The importance of teachers' emotions and instructional behavior for their students' emotions – an experience sampling analysis. *Teaching and Teacher Education, 43*, 15–26. (Quote on p. 22). https://doi.org/10.1016/j.tate.2014.05.002; Kim, L.E., Dar-Nimrod, I., & MacCann, C. (2018). Teacher personality and teacher effectiveness in secondary

school: Personality predicts teacher support and student self-efficacy but not academic achievement. *Journal of Educational Psychology, 110*(3), 309–323.

4 Jung, C. G. (2010). *Synchronicity: An acausal connecting principle.* Princeton: Princeton University Press.

5 Blackburn, E., & Epel, E. (2017). *The telomere effect.* New York: Grand Central Publishing.

6 Schutte, N. S., Malouff, J. M., & Keng, S. (2020). Meditation and telomere length: A meta-analysis. *Psychol.Health, 35*(8), 901–915. https://doi.org/10.1080/08870446.2019.1707827; Mendioroz, M., Puebla-Guedea, M., Montero-Marin, J., Urdanoz-Casado, A., Blanco-Luquin, I., Roldan, M., Labarga, A., & Garcia-Campayo, J. (2020). Telomere length correlates with subtelomeric DNA methylation in long-term mindfulness practioners. *Scientific Reports, 10*(4564); Keng, S., Looi, P. S., Tan, E. L. Y., Yim, O., Lai, P. S., Chew, S. H., & Ebstein, R. P. (2020). Effects of mindfulness-based stress reduction on psychological symptoms and telomere length: A randomized active-controlled trial. *Behavior Therapy, 51*(6), 984–996. https://doi.org/10.1016/j.beth.2020.01.005

7 Jung, C. G. (2010). *Synchronicity: An acausal connecting principle.* Princeton: Princeton University Press. p. 25.

8 Ibid. p. 21.

Part III

Shifting Your Energy

Simple Strategies to Introduce Mindfulness into Your Life Now

15

Shifting Your Energy and the Energy of Your Classroom

Mindfully Creating Your Classroom or Workspace

Not ready to learn meditation or jump into a regular mindfulness practice? Or perhaps you aren't currently able to incorporate mindfulness techniques into your classroom or work setting. That's okay. There are a few simple things that anyone can do immediately, without any training in mindfulness, to begin to improve the energy of their classroom or work environment. These tips are easy and can be applied in just about any setting. I have found that by creating a more harmonious classroom setting, both the teacher and the students will function in a healthier, happier manner.

The Physical Space of the Room

I'm an amateur feng shui practitioner, and by amateur, I mean that I've read some books about it and have had actual feng shui experts come to my home to advise me on the layout, colors, and placement of things like mirrors and plants and the symbolic placement of pictures and other décor. In my own crude way, I will define feng shui as how energy flows in and out of a space. Feng shui is an ancient Chinese practice that is multidimensional and quite intricate. At its very basic level of meaning, feng shui is the art of designing a space to maximize its positive energy and minimize negative energy. The words feng shui literally mean "wind and water."[1] Author and feng shui expert Lillian Too explains that "Feng shui is an ancient Chinese science, which prescribes ways of living in a state of harmony and balance with your personal environment."[2] Since learning about feng shui years ago, I have tried to apply its basic principles to both my home and my classroom. For me, feng shui is simply a way to be mindful of how you arrange and create your living and working space.

Furniture Arrangement

In my classroom, I was limited in what I could do in terms of feng shui because I couldn't move the location of my room or repaint it, for instance. However, there were a few simple things I could do to help enhance the positive atmosphere and flow of the room. My rudimentary understanding of feng shui allowed me to acknowledge the importance of creating a space that felt warm and inviting. Arranging the desks in a harmonious way was something that I was able to do to allow easy movement between the desks and clear paths around the room. It might seem obvious, but desks should be arranged in such a way that people are easily able to walk around all areas of the room, and no student should feel like they are trapped against a wall.

I also think allowing all of the desks to face the front of the room and the door is important. Even though everyone might not be directly facing the door, everyone should be able to see the door from where they are sitting. And nobody should be made to sit with their back to the door. Sitting with one's back toward a door can be quite unsettling, even if just subconsciously. Everywhere I go, I try to avoid sitting with my back toward the door. For my own desk in the classroom, I moved it to the back corner of the room (still with a direct site line to the door) so that I could see who was coming in my room before they could see me. It gave me a sense of comfort and safety. When I first rearranged my classroom and placed my desk in the back, I think other teachers thought it was rather strange, but then I started to notice some other teachers doing the same thing. Placing the desk in the back, gave me a wonderful vantage point to see everything that was going on in the room as well. I suggest experimenting with the placement of your desk and the students' desks and just sit with it to see how it makes you *feel*. Do you feel comfortable? Safe? Aware of all parts of the room?

I've come up with a *very* informal theory on connecting where students sit in the room to their behavior. I don't know why exactly but it always seemed that certain desks created (or attracted?) certain personalities. I would make jokes about this in class. A student would be acting all goofy, and I would say, "It's okay. It's not you. It's the seat. Same thing happens in every class. The seat makes you act goofy" (or cranky…or confused…or chatty…or whatever the behavior was). It was such a seemingly off-the-wall response to students' behavior that we'd all laugh, and it would instantly dispel any tension. But it's rather bizarrely true. In so many instances, it seemed that students would behave in certain ways based on where they sat in the room. Could this be just a coincidence? Maybe. It's strange, though. I would continue to see certain patterns year after year that seemed to match the seat with certain personalities. Could students somehow be responding to how they felt or how they were able to pay attention in a certain space?

By the way, this power of how a physical space can influence people applies to any business or work setting, not just schools. Here's a quick example. At my husband's business, there was an office space that no employee lasted very long in. They would hire someone and place that person in that office, and before long that person would quit or be fired for some reason. This kept happening. It wasn't even the same position that these people were hired for. Whoever was given this office to work out of for any position never lasted very long in the company. And it wasn't because it wasn't a nice office. In fact, it was a big office with windows—quite nice looking really. It became a joke around the office. (Hey, if the company wants to get rid of you, you'll know because they'll put you in *the* office.) Finally, they decided to repurpose the space for something else, and the retention rate of the new hires completely changed for the better.

In terms of my classroom space, I had a very small room and had only just enough seats for students in many of my classes, so I wasn't always able to be too selective regarding where students sat. For smaller classes, I could strategically avoid the seats that might not have been the best or that seemed to "attract" disruptive students. Every physical space will have its own personality, so I can't tell you that a specific seat will result in a particular behavior or characteristic in your room. Just see if you can start to become aware of this phenomenon in your own room. Do you notice any patterns? If you do have options of rearranging your room or playing with seating configurations, you can have fun trying different options. It's also a good idea to actually sit and pretend to be a student in different seats around the room, so that you can really get a sense of what the student can see from that seat and how the student might feel sitting there. Again, like I mentioned with my husband's work setting, this phenomenon of where someone sits or works doesn't apply just to schools. It can apply to any office or place of business.

Adding Some Nature

Another easy idea for improving the energy of your classroom is to add plants. I am always happy when I go into a teacher's room and see plants. The use of plants in a classroom pulls in nature and helps to make the room feel less institutional. Plants add a softness and warmth to the room. Plants are also natural air purifiers. There are many plants that are helpful for reducing toxins in the air. If you are like me and don't have a green thumb, there are two indoor plants that I have had great success with: the spider plant and the snake plant. Both are touted for their ability to purify the air, and I've been able to keep both alive for a very long time!

If you don't have windows in your classroom, even putting pictures of nature scenes around the room can help. Images of nature can help to achieve a soothing effect on the mind and body. I think it's interesting how there's been this emergence of belief in the power of "forest bathing." It seems like one of these new mindfulness concepts, but really it's just getting back to our roots as living beings connected to the earth. When we walk in nature surrounded by trees, our energy shifts. Forest bathing helps to wash away our stress, allowing us to emerge a little lighter and refreshed. If we can't be in an actual forest, at least seeing images of trees and nature can evoke a bit of those feelings.

Recently, I spent time visiting my dad in the hospital after he had major surgery. The hospital had just undergone a renovation, and I was so happy to see that throughout the lobbies, waiting rooms, and hallways, there were beautiful photographs of nature scenes. The images included flowers, trees, and meadows. All of the pictures evoked a sense of serenity and calm. Even though it was a stressful time for me and my family, these photos really did make me smile as we walked through the corridors and sat waiting for hours. The hospital clearly understood the power of nature to help in the healing process and to help soothe those experiencing a stressful time.

Visuals

Speaking of *what* we see influencing *how* we feel, the visuals that are around the classroom are important to consider. Undoubtedly, there are going to be posters and signs that pertain to the content being taught or to school policies. But what else can there be for students to see on a daily basis? Teachers have a wonderful opportunity to positively convey messages to students—even subconsciously—just by what they put around the classroom. Every day, students are sitting in the room and looking around, and whether they realize it or not, they are being influenced by the messaging on the walls. Placing inspirational quotes and images around the room is an easy way to contribute to a more positive tone of the classroom. Be mindful of the kinds of messages and visuals that you and your students are ingesting on a regular basis.

Music

Music is another easy way to create a tone of happiness and lightness in the room. I would start my classes by playing a song as the students entered the room. I had the song on repeat mode, so that it played for the entire five minutes between classes that students would stagger into the room. The songs were basic pop songs that had some sort of positive, motivational message to them. Sometimes I would reference the song we were listening to at the start of class, and sometimes I would just let it go without saying anything about it. I would hear students talk about the song some days. Or there were times when I would play certain songs that related to the theme of a piece of literature we were studying. I would ask students to pay close attention to the lyrics, and that would be a springboard for our discussion on the literature. Music is a powerful vehicle for shifting how we feel. Being intentional about what I played for my students not only helped to set the tone of the class but also opened doors for rich discussions.

On a side note, I don't suggest just playing music in the background as students are reading or working. I know that some people find music being played in the background relaxing or motivational, but for some students, having music on while they are trying to focus can be a serious distraction. I remember a friend telling me that she had this young, cool teacher who thought it would be nice to play music while students were working, and my friend said that she wasn't able to concentrate on the assignment. I asked her why she didn't just tell the teacher that she couldn't focus and to please shut off the music. She said that she was too embarrassed to say anything. She didn't want to be the reason why the rest of the class (who all *seemed* to like the music) couldn't listen to it. My suggestion: music is great for the beginning and end of a class period, but during times when students have to read or write, keep it off. Don't ask if the class wants to listen to music or not, because like the example I just shared, the shy kid or the kid who really struggles to focus is not going to be comfortable going against what they perceive to be the majority.

First Impressions

How class is started each day is critically important. I used to roll my eyes at administration when they insisted that teachers be in the doorway between classes. There was so much to do! I couldn't just stand there. I had to shift gears between two different classes and get ready for the next lesson. *But* what I discovered is that greeting students in the doorway as they enter really is the best way to make personal connections with each student and set the tone for the class period. Sometimes I would have to run across the hall to the restroom first, but then I'd come back and greet students. In those couple of minutes, I could ask a student how their track meet went or if their boss agreed to give them time off for the school dance or how they did on the math test they were dreading. I could ask them how their older sister was doing or compliment their hair cut or take notice of their new shoes.

The point is that with each student who entered the room, I could make a personal connection and let them know that I remembered what was going on in their lives outside of my class. These were quick conversations or comments, but in this short exchange, I could see if there was something "off" with a particular student. I could sometimes offer a quick bit of advice or offer for the student to follow up with me after class or during lunch if there was a larger issue that they expressed. Most of the time, this quick greeting at the door just set the tone for a more positive classroom atmosphere. I have found that students are less likely to be disruptive in class and are more likely to participate in a constructive manner when a personal connection has been made.

Smile ☺

Smile. It's so easy, and still so many people can't do it. Or they won't do it. Maybe people don't realize the power of a smile. I have found that when I smile at somebody, they usually soften, sometimes they even smile back. Smiling is a de-escalation tool.

A grumpy face can escalate a stressful situation or at the very least do nothing to help, whereas smiling allows the humanity to enter, and it doesn't cost anything! It's totally free and takes almost no effort. Mother Teresa, who spent her life performing selfless acts of compassion, was an advocate for smiling. I learned about Mother Teresa's wisdom from one of my best friends in college, who worked with Mother Teresa in India. Mother Teresa worked in some of the worst conditions in the world and saw tremendous suffering. In her wisdom to help make the world a better place, she advised people to *smile*. She has been quoted many times regarding the importance of smiling. Even if I was too busy to have a long conversation with a student, I could always very quickly smile and say "Good morning!"

BOX 15.1   Smile Exercise

A Quick Exercise

Interestingly, when you smile, it affects not just the people around you. It affects *you*. Smiling does something to your body. Take a second and smile right now. Really smile. If you're not used to doing this, you might need to think about a really happy moment you've experienced or think about someone you really love. Either way, right now break out into a big smile. Try it. Smile. Hold it for a moment. How do you feel? Do you notice anything shifting in your body? Do you notice any sensations in your body? Maybe you begin to feel a release of stress? Maybe you begin to sense a subtle surge of happiness? When you smile, you are connecting the mind and body, and the simple act of smiling can generate the releasing of feel-good endorphins.[3]

If you feel inauthentic about smiling, just keep trying it! If this quick exercise that you can do pretty much anywhere throughout your day feels awkward to you, then you definitely need to work on smiling more! Eventually, smiling will become more natural to you and will become more genuine. Smiling is one of the best ways to shift your energy and the energy of your environment.

Grandma's Pantry

I had the privilege of growing up with an old-fashioned grandma who was always cooking and baking. My grandparents lived close to us, so at least several times a week, we went over to visit. My brother and I would run through the front door, which was never locked, and run straight into the kitchen, straight to the cookie jar. Ah, the cookie jar. As an adult, I can't imagine just having a jar of cookies on my counter at all times. It seems like the cookie jar and the candy dish have become lost symbols of a slower time just hanging out with the grandparents on a Sunday.

The cookie jar wasn't just the container of a sugary snack. It represented the love and generosity of my grandma. It symbolized her wanting to make all of her kids and grandkids feel welcome in her home. On the few occasions when the cookie jar was found empty, my grandma would profusely apologize and usually blame one of my uncles for scarfing down all of the cookies. The cookie jar consistently being there for us with a yummy treat was something that we could all depend upon. It was there to cheer us up or to celebrate a good grade on a test. It provided comfort and assurance throughout our childhood.

This is why I created my own "grandma's pantry" in my classroom. I didn't necessarily advertise this to my students, but anytime a student needed something, I just quietly opened my cupboard and found all sorts of snacks and supplies. Then, often without saying anything to the student, I would just silently, casually put whatever they needed on their desk and continue teaching. There were times when I would hear a student say they were really hungry to another student, or a student would tell me that they missed breakfast and then I would give them a snack. Sometimes I just sensed that something was off with a student and then I would nonchalantly put a snack on their desk. They would look up at me and smile. If they didn't want it, they could exchange it for a different snack or give it to someone else. There were times when I would offer the entire class a piece of candy too. Students never took advantage of the treats or made a mess with them. They were always appreciative of the kindness.

I would always keep a box of tissues out in the classroom for students to grab whenever they needed them. Occasionally, I would get annoyed when I would see students grabbing handfuls of tissues and jamming them in their pockets. But then they would say that my room was the only class they had all day that had tissues, and they needed some for later because of having a cold or allergies. I was annoyed with their other teachers, but I then understood why they took so many. Most of my career, the school did not provide tissues for classrooms, so I had to purchase these and other "non-essential" supplies myself.

I also kept hand lotion on the counter in my room. Students were very glad to have this available. Word got out that I had hand lotion for students in my room, and I would find students whom I didn't even teach stopping in my room and asking if they could use some because their hands were so dry from washing, especially in the winter months. These simple gestures of kindness made a big difference in how students perceived my classroom and me.

In terms of the snacks that I kept in the room, they were nut-free, and I would always ask about any allergies. At the high school level, students were old enough to know what they could and could not eat and would let me know. For elementary students, I would have reached out to the parents at the start of the year to get approval.

BOX 15.2   List of Classroom Pantry Items

Grandma's Pantry
- A variety of snacks such as pretzels, crackers, and granola bars
- Juice boxes
- Sewing kit, including safety pins
- Gently used notebooks, binders, and pens/pencils
- Bandages
- Tissues
- Paper towels (the kind provided in schools are usually horrible and don't absorb anything)
- Hand lotion

Bottom Line

A general rule that guided me in my approach to creating my classroom atmosphere was simple: Would I like to be a student in this class? How would I feel if I had to sit here for 45 minutes each day? How would I like a teacher to treat me? What might take away from or add to my learning in this space?

Once I had children of my own, I started to ask similar questions but through the eyes of my kids and their distinct personalities. Would this be a good environment for my kids to be in? To learn in? To feel safe in? How would I want a teacher to treat *my* kids?

Learning to become more aware of any space whether it's a classroom, a business, a home, an exercise studio, or an office can be life-transforming. Every space has a certain energy, and in many cases, we have the power to change what that energy is—either good or not so good. By understanding the basic principles of practices such as feng shui or just by becoming in tune with how a space *feels* to us, we can apply easy strategies to improve both the physical space and the energetic quality of our work and home environments. Our own actions, such as the simple act of smiling, can also alter the energy of our surroundings.

Notes

1 Wydra, N. (1993). *Feng shui the book of cures: 150 simple solutions for health and happiness in your home or office.* Chicago: Contemporary Books.
2 Too, L. (1998). *Essential feng shui: A step-by-step guide to enhancing your relationships, health, and prosperity.* New York: Ballantine Wellspring. p. 6.
3 Bloom, W. (2001). *The endorphin effect: A breakthrough strategy for holistic health and spiritual wellbeing.* London: Piatkus.

16

Suggestions for Learning to Meditate and Incorporating a Mindfulness Program into a School or Workplace

Want to Try Meditation Yourself?

If after reading about the many physical and mental health benefits of meditation, you are thinking that maybe you would like to try it, then the most important piece of advice I can give you is to find a credentialed, highly experienced meditation teacher. The ideal meditation teacher should have a personal meditation practice that they have been consistent with for many years and should be certified to teach through a meditation program that is structured and vetted and offers face-to-face, real-time instruction for at least a portion of the program. I practiced meditation for 10 years before I trained to become a meditation teacher.

Some meditation programs offer several face-to-face meetings to learn their type of meditation, and some programs offer 8-week courses in which different formal and informal mindfulness techniques are taught. I am certified in two different forms of meditation: The one type is the Vedic form of meditation that is taught on an individual basis and requires the student to meet face-to-face with a certified instructor two or three times for about 1.5 to 2 hours each time. The other type is a mindfulness-based meditation program that is taught in a small group setting over the course of eight weeks. The eight-week course can be taught remotely, but it must be live, real-time instruction, not through video recordings. There are a number of meditation programs you can look into to see which one is the best fit for you and your lifestyle. But again, just be sure that there is actual real-time, face-to-face instruction with a highly trained meditation teacher as part of the program.

Can't I Just Use a Mindfulness/Meditation App?

This is a common question. We now use apps for *everything*. Mostly, they are extremely helpful. We have come to rely on them for banking, for checking our kids' grades, for the weather, for exercising, for figuring out what to eat—for basically everything we do. We have given our lives over to our phones. Some people even use their phones to tell them when it's time to go to bed. This amuses me. Just like we are children again and can't figure out a reasonable time to go to bed, we now need our phone to be the responsible adult in our lives and tell us it's "nighty-night" time.

So it seems only natural to assume that an app can take over our ability to train our minds and to learn to relax. Why not? I'll invite you to sit for a moment and think about what you believe could be the pros and cons of relying on an app to find inner peace and to tap into the deeper levels of your consciousness.

A few years ago, I would have never made this argument. However, with the insidious expansion of artificial intelligence, I think that it does warrant at least a brief questioning of whether or not it's wise that we hand over the very basics of living to an outside agency, so to speak. Whereas the rest of our lives are largely controlled through technology, our minds or our consciousness is really the final frontier left for us to explore and to control freely. Instead of mindlessly clicking on an app and expecting it to train our minds and relax us, we should mindfully learn how to do this on our own. Our tendency is to take the path of least resistance and do whatever is easiest, but what is easiest might not be the best.

I'm not alone in questioning the merits of relying on an app to learn meditation or mindfulness. According to Terry Hyland, a prolific writer and teacher of mindfulness, "the numerous mindfulness apps and products…are—not simply ludicrous and exploitative mutations of mindfulness—but positively harmful to health in that they mislead people and construct obstacles to the sort of mindfulness transformation conducive to mind/body well-being."[1]

After learning how to meditate through a *real* teacher and having a personal connection with that accredited meditation teacher, then by all means, feel free to try some of the mindfulness apps for some additional relaxation. Also, many mindfulness programs will give you a free app you can download and/or free recordings to use with your practices based on their teachings. These are legitimate resources that have been created by experienced, highly trained instructors. This gives you the best of both worlds. The key is to have an actual teacher that you can connect with anytime you have questions or need additional support. However, there are some forms of meditation that are based on ancient practices that will not succumb to the trend of using an app for their teachings since what they offer is a profoundly effective technique that adheres to the belief in the sacred connection between teacher and student. We must acknowledge that these practices have been successful for thousands of years and can offer us benefits that no app can.

Want to Introduce Mindfulness to Your Students or Co-Workers?

If you want to introduce mindfulness practices to your classroom, school, or company, there are a few important things to be aware of, including ethical considerations and the potential concerns for individuals who have experienced trauma. First and foremost, any mindfulness or meditation program must be completely voluntary. No program should ever be forced upon anyone, whether it be in a school or a work setting. That being said, I believe that everyone in a school, health-care organization, or work setting should be *introduced* to mindfulness/meditation, and schools and organizations can make it mandatory to attend the *introductory session*. This way, everyone can learn about what mindfulness or meditation is and what the overall benefits might be for them. Everyone will then have the basic information to make an informed decision regarding whether or not they want to learn more about mindfulness. Then, after the introductory session, it has to be optional for students or employees. Opting out of these programs must be easy. In fact, really it should be set up as an "opt in" approach rather than an "opt out" approach, so that nobody is made to feel ashamed or defiant for not wanting to be part of the program. The other reason for the "opt in" approach is to be able to focus on people who are genuinely interested in learning and participating in these practices during the training.

In a school setting, this idea of mindfulness being optional is extremely important. Sometimes we oversimplify the idea of mindfulness and readily believe that every student could be benefitting from it. However, there is a level of readiness on the part of the student. According to the U.S. Department of Health and Human Services, more than two thirds of children reported at least one traumatic event by age 16.[2] As a teacher, you may already know some of the students sitting in your room who have experienced a traumatic event; however, I can guarantee that you don't know all of the students who have experienced a past trauma. That's why it's so important to proceed with caution when introducing mindfulness to your classes. If you or your school is interested in adopting a mindfulness program, I highly recommend that you read David A. Treleaven's book *Trauma-Sensitive Mindfulness: Practices for Safe and Transformative Healing*.[3] When we practice mindfulness, we are looking inward.

We are bringing awareness to our bodies and our minds. Not everyone is ready to do this.

In schools, it is highly recommended that counselors and therapists from the district be aware of any potential mindfulness program being introduced and that these professionals become part of the process. They can be on standby in case a student needs to discuss their feelings or any adverse reaction. Release forms should also be part of the process. Not all schools have permission slips required for students to be part of a mindfulness program, but I really believe that for ethical purposes, the parent or guardian should be aware of the program and should have to give their consent. For adult populations, if someone is under any type of psychiatric care, the provider should also be made aware of the program and should sign off on their patient being ready to practice mindfulness or meditation. At the very least, the participant should sign a form acknowledging that the mindfulness program is not intended to diagnose or treat physical or mental health conditions.

Alternatives for Students

There are two main options for students who select not to participate in a mindfulness practice at school. One, an alternative space can be provided for students to report to during the mindfulness practice. There may be logistical issues, however, with having an extra room available, having staff to monitor the students, and having a meaningful activity for the students to do during this time. The second option, which is more practical and is advocated by the Mindfulness-Based Living Course for Young Adults that I teach, is to have students all in the same room. All students can have the opportunity to hear the introduction to a particular mindfulness technique; then for the actual practice component, students can either decide to try the technique or select another activity such as mindful coloring, drawing, or word puzzles. So that students don't feel put on the spot at the start of the mindfulness technique, the instructor should have these alternate activities already placed on all of the students' desks or tables at the start of the lesson. That way, students don't have to get up and call attention to themselves if they decide that they don't want to participate. Any student who doesn't wish to participate for any reason can still be in the room and be able to listen to the mindfulness practice while they are doing another activity silently. Then, if at any point they feel comfortable with trying the practice, they can silently jump in and try the practice with the rest of the class. Likewise, if a student started the practice and part way through becomes uncomfortable, they can just as easily stop the practice and silently and discreetly begin to do one of the other activities that are already at their seats.

In mindfulness classes, there is usually some type of feedback or inquiry component at the end of each practice. In adult groups, this is usually done in small groups followed by a whole-group, instructor-led discussion. However, with students, it might be uncomfortable for them to share their feelings and what they experienced during a mindfulness practice, so it's advised to use alternate strategies such as journaling or have students respond to a question (or questions) on a piece of paper that they can fold up and hand to the instructor.

Additional Guidelines

Clearly, there is a good deal to consider before jumping into a mindfulness program in any setting. This is why I cringe a little when I hear about a school or a teacher saying that they are using mindfulness with their students. I immediately wonder if they are qualified to teach mindfulness and if they have taken the necessary steps to ensure that students have a healthy and beneficial experience and that ethical considerations have been addressed.

> **BOX 16.1 Additional Guidelines for Mindfulness Programs in Schools**
>
> **Here Are a Few Guidelines**
>
> - Whoever is teaching mindfulness needs to be qualified. This includes classroom teachers. The person doing the instruction needs to have practiced themselves, and they need to have formal training in teaching mindfulness. The high school I taught in invited an outside group to conduct mindfulness training with our students. The one instructor sat in front of my class, rang a meditation bell, and told the students to just breathe. She then told me that she's never really practiced mindfulness before and didn't know much about it. She had just learned about it a few months ago.
> - Practices should be kept to an age-appropriate, developmentally aware length. Practices should be shorter than regular, formal mindfulness practices.
> - Some may argue that there is a concern about cultural appropriation of mindfulness practices. It's important to acknowledge that although the practices done in schools or work settings are secular and designed for health and well-being, there should also be transparency in acknowledging the Buddhist foundations of mindfulness.
> - Teachers must be aware of possible adverse effects of mindfulness practice—especially with people who have any experiences of trauma. Mindfulness can be therapeutic for trauma survivors, but it can also have the adverse effects of triggering past trauma. Encourage students to talk to their counselor or therapist.
> - Not everyone is going to have the same experience with every mindfulness practice. There's no one "right" way to feel during or after a practice. Students should know that they haven't failed in doing a mindfulness practice just because they might not feel as relaxed as somebody else, for instance.
> - There is an ethical and legal obligation to report any indication of abuse or neglect that a student might disclose during or after a mindfulness lesson.

BOX 16.2 Creating a Safe Space for Teaching Mindfulness

Creating a Safe Space for Mindfulness Teaching

- In school settings, the classroom teacher must always be in the room during the lesson or practice. Even if another instructor comes in to conduct the mindfulness sessions, the actual classroom teacher *must* be present at all times. There are a number of reasons for this. The regular classroom teacher knows each student and his or her needs and behaviors. The regular classroom teacher can provide support and help to redirect students. If there is an issue, the regular teacher can take a student out of the room and talk with them individually. Also, it's a good idea for the classroom teacher to know what the class is learning, so that they can refer to the lesson at another time.
- When guiding a mindfulness practice, avoid speaking in directives; rather, use suggestions. For example, instead of saying "Sit up straight and breathe in," we may say "Seeing what it feels like to sit with a straight back. Noticing the breath moving in and out of the body... Breathing however it feels most comfortable for you."
- *Scent-Free Environment.* This is so often overlooked. I am a staunch advocate for avoiding things like air fresheners in classrooms. This is for a number of reasons, including the effects on students with allergies, chemical sensitivities, migraines, or seizure disorders. For trauma survivors, scent can be a significant trigger of traumatic memories. Avoid perfume, cologne, air fresheners, scented laundry detergents, and so on.[4]
- It might be obvious, but there should be *no* physical contact.
- Not everyone is going to be comfortable closing their eyes during a mindfulness practice. Instead of saying "Close your eyes," tell students that if they are comfortable closing their eyes, they can, or they can just look down at their desks or laps.
- The instructor's eyes should always remain open during the mindfulness practice to be fully aware of what is going on in the room and to see if any student needs anything.

Bringing It All Together

Now that I've addressed some of the ways you can help to ensure that you and others have a safe, beneficial experience with mindfulness and meditation, I want to acknowledge the power of these practices. With proper training, meditation and mindfulness can transform your life in the most magnificent of ways. Meditating benefits not only the individual but also those around them because the qualities of compassion (including self-compassion), kindness, creativity, and wisdom grow through the regular practice of meditation. Meditation is a salve to soothe daily struggles while cultivating creative problem-solving.

As a result of meditating, I have experienced a deepening of life. I have an understanding and appreciation for living that extend beyond the surface of merely existing from day to day. There is more of a depth to my interactions with others and the world around me. I *feel* better, happier, and lighter. Insight and awareness emerge from the stillness of meditation, and through this, I have discovered that meditating has given me the edge throughout my career as a teacher and throughout all aspects of my life.

I wish the same for you.

Notes

1 Hyland, T. (2017). McDonaldizing spirituality: Mindfulness, education, and consumerism. *Journal of Transformative Education, 15*(4), 334–356. (p. 344–345) doi:10.1177/1541344617696972
2 U.S. Department of Health & Human Services, 2022.
3 Treleaven, D. A. (2018). *Trauma-sensitive mindfulness: Practices for safe and transformative healing*. New York: Norton.
4 Ibid.